www.unlimited-success.co.uk

Order this book online at www.unlimited-success.co.uk
or on Amazon.co.uk

Note for Librarians: A cataloguing record for this book is available from Library and Archives Canada at www.collections Canada.ca/amicus/index-e.html

A catalogue record for this book is available from the British Library:
ISBN: 978-1-909846-56-2

Printed in Peterborough, Cambridgeshire, UK

ISBN: 978-1-909846-56-2
www.unlimited-success.co.uk
Unlimited Success
Unit 9 Forder Way
Cygnet Park
Peterborough
PE7 8GX
01733 898550
hello@unlimited-success.co.uk

WEALTH
DNA

Daniel Wagner

Dedication

Thank you - you know who you are.

Wealth DNA

'That's Just Who I Am'

"That's just who I am." The five most damaging words ever spoken. Because you do not believe that you can change. You become a victim. You blame circumstances. You complain about the hand you've been given. You justify your current status – not just financial status, but the state of your health, the state of your relationships and the state of your wealth. I call this "living below the line." You have a list of excuses of why your life isn't going how or where you want it to. And most of my life I lived below the line. I made up all kinds of reasons (excuses) why I couldn't be happy, healthy or wealthy.

You see, if you were with me on a Friday night in late November 2004, at 1 A.M., you'd be sitting beside me in a white beaten-up Skoda 120L, which I bought for £100 (and it was worth every penny). You'd be wearing a blue Domino's pizza uniform and delivering a medium Tandoori hot to one of the most notorious council estates in Slough. It was the last delivery of the night, and I was almost done, and this pizza was for one of my regulars. Marco was a scruffy, skinny minor who was half my age, but his arrogance made me question everything about myself. But he always tipped me a pound, sometimes two. I knew he was dealing drugs, but I was complicit in his petty crime because he was one of my best tippers. Whenever he opened the door he always just wore dirty white pants with his ribcage puffed out, and the stench from the house would smack me so hard in the face I could get stoned on the backdraft. His posse that I could see from outside would snigger at a man nearly 40 years of age delivering pizzas in a dirty blue uniform and baseball cap. I could muster a smile because the "happy pizza boy" would get better tips, but inside I was crying and ashamed.

How did a good guy, hard working and by no means stupid, end up here? Every night when I got home to my wife and kids I would have made £5 an hour, 50p a pizza and tips for smiling at people mocking me. I felt embarrassed, trapped and unworthy. I didn't feel like a man; I felt like a loser, a pushover.

I didn't believe in having a "soul," but I always wondered what people meant by "selling your soul." Now I understood: it means doing something that compromises who you are - your integrity - for money, something that makes you feel worthless, like smiling when you want to cry to get a £1 tip. Something that eats away at your character day by day, until you wake up age forty and you have nothing. And the worst part about that nothing is that it isn't just the physical nothing, the lack of material things, but the self-worth of nothing.

I felt like society had cast me aside. But I also felt powerless to change it. I'd look at my wife Clare each night, whom I had promised to give a good life, and I'd feel that I'd let her down. That I'd failed the promise of our marriage. I'd look at my two young children, whom I so badly wanted to give the best opportunities in life, and I'd feel like a failure because I hadn't.

And I'd look at myself – three stone overweight, totally broke and in debt, living in one room with my wife and two kids, drinking a bottle of pink Pepto-Bismol each night and having to sleep upright to stop acid reflux – and I just wanted to hide from my own life.

But there was no hiding place from myself. The tiny room I lived in with my wife and kids was in a shared house called an Ashram (a spiritual commune) with fourteen people, all belonging to my religious group following an Indian "Guru" that many would call a cult.

Although we all believed it was conducive to our spiritual practice, it was also a very cheap way to live and the only way I could afford to get by. At this stage I'd dedicated sixteen years of my life to "spirituality," cutting myself off completely from outside society, feeling that poverty was spiritual and wealth would be a "blessing of Lakshmi." I believed that because the world and its monetary economy would come to an end; accumulation would be irrelevant, unnecessary and a waste of time. Modesty and humility meant dedication, and wealth and money meant being wasteful, ostentatious and selfish.

I'd adopted someone else's philosophy of life because mine had totally previously so blatantly failed me. I became a follower and gave up my right or ability to question the Guru's omnipotent "wisdom." At the beginning that felt comforting because I didn't have to make my own decisions, but over time this became restrictive and suffocating.

When the group saved me from my drug addiction at age twenty-one, I was of course grateful. I had been an addict for years, trying everything in my power to change my self-destructive behaviour. And I had failed. Again and again. In the end I looked for help outside. The spiritual group seemed to promise me everything I was looking for: support, community, a clear set of rules and a leader that told me what to do.

And it wasn't just a philosophy of what was right and wrong, but a philosophy of my entire life. My marriage to Clare was arranged by the Guru, when I'd asked him to pick me a partner. I had to fill in a one-page form about myself and trust the Guru to pick my soul mate. I was so unsure about myself and what I wanted that I relinquished responsibility of my key life decisions to my Guru. It was a real badge of honour in the group and showed full dedication to send your kids to the group's schools. So at age three I sent my kids away to

Rome to the designated pre-school, and at age six I sent them to the main school for the group in the Himalayas in India, where the next generation of Yogis and spiritual world leaders would be groomed.

And I am ashamed to admit that in one way I was quite relieved that the burden of fatherhood was no longer solely on my shoulders, as I didn't feel I could or wanted to handle the responsibility, and at the same time I could carry the kudos of the "most dedicated Yogi." Looking back it seems so crazy to think that I was a passenger of my own life, and although my case is somewhat extreme, I feel that so many people I meet today have also just become passengers to their own lives, watching as their lives pass them by.

I generally don't do regrets, but one of my life's regrets is missing out on the precious time with my kids and the unique experiences I missed out on that I can never bring back. And all because I didn't take the responsibility when I had the chance.

You might question how and why I ended up in the group in the first place.

Weirdly, I had a charmed childhood up until age fourteen. I was good at everything, popular, the life of the party. School was easy, I had top grades in every subject without even trying and, because of this, I got a lot of love from my mum. And my three years older sister Karin didn't. She tried so hard, but whatever she tried wasn't good enough. I was the golden boy, and it was hurting my sister. At this point in my life I wasn't fully aware or conscious of the situation, but I unearthed it in later sessions of self- discovery.

So I started to act up. I dismantled the perfect image of Daniel and became the bad boy. I missed a lot of classes, got into drugs and petty crime and had many meaningless, womanising relationships through my late teens. In an act of ultimate rebellion I even tried to burn the school down! I thought if I became really bad, my sister would look better, get more attention and therefore get more love from my mum. As I pushed the boundaries further and further my life spiralled out of control. I had become a drug addict and lost control of my life. I was so desperately searching for meaning and guidance. And at age twenty, after three years lost in the wilderness, I finally found the spiritual group and the structure and safety I so badly craved to help me battle my addiction.

So here I was, age forty. Ex-drug addict, cult member, broke, overweight, sick, unhappy, unfulfilled, a failure to my wife and kids -- this was my CV to apply for my new life of wealth and happiness. Would you have given me a chance? But all through this time, these two decades of the most important time in my life, I secretly wanted to be wealthy. I was afraid to admit it because I was afraid to fail and to appear superficial and non-spiritual, afraid to be ridiculed by my peers and my family; I guess the irony was that my fear of failing of becoming rich and wealthy was that everything in my life was a failure anyway. I couldn't have looked like a bigger loser. I felt that my life was a joke and a living nightmare.

Fast forward to now and I am financially free, happily (re)married, the healthiest I've ever been. I live a life of purpose doing what I love and making great money. If you were to meet me now and ask me how I am, my response is always the same: "I'm living the dream, my friend, living the dream." Just to be clear though - I don't intend for this book to brag of how many multi-millions I make or be a trumpet-blowing autobiography; the only purpose of sharing my story (apart from you thinking you had it quite good) is that I want to share with you the massive change I experienced in my life once I learned the laws of wealth and money. I'm not Richard Branson, but life today is amazing. I have a seven-figure property portfolio that produces a six-figure rent roll. My different e-commerce businesses turn over almost seven figures, and my small business (which has just one employee, by design) is also turning over seven figures a year. I work when I want, where I want with whomever I want. I had nine holidays this year alone, pretty much all of them on business expenses, and as I write this book I am with my wife in Dubai in the Atlantis hotel, one of the most amazing hotels in the world, getting air miles for all my spending! I'm in my best health and energy ever, having self-cured my illnesses through better knowledge of nutrition and lifestyle choices. I am recently married to the love of my life, I have repaired the relationships with my children and act out gratitude every day. I feel excited for every new day and love to learn, develop and grow to become a better person and achieve more and give more.

There is good chance you never heard of me, but if you had, it'd be most likely for my work as an international speaker on Entrepreneurial success. Since 2006 I have trained and inspired 10,000s of people helping them become financially free, teaching them the mindset and skill set of success, helping them overcome the same challenges I had, giving them belief that they can do it too.

I am certainly not the richest man in the world. I don't need to be, though I won't stop aspiring to acquire more. Many have more material riches than me. But I feel truly wealthy. And I truly believe that anyone can change their life for the better. Starting now. Anyone can become wealthy despite their past, their failures and their upbringing. Anyone can change what I call their Wealth DNA.

After all, I am living proof. And I will do my best to show you more proof and real-world examples later in the book. There was no one I know less qualified or in my mind less deserving of wealth than me, no one with a worse Wealth DNA. Yet in a few short years I have turned it around, turned me around, against the odds and self- sabotage, to live a wealthy life beyond my own expectations and dreams.

"That's just who I am" wasn't true. It wasn't in my DNA to be broke and unhappy, sick and overweight. I wasn't born that way so I didn't have to live that way. I was able to break the poverty code with what I now know to be the proven principles of lasting wealth. I changed my debilitating beliefs, I became a student of wealth and not a follower of a Guru, I invested as much time and money I had into myself instead of hoping for handouts and I created my own philosophy instead of just accepting and following someone else's. I now trust myself to choose my own partners in life and in business. Instead of waiting for things to change, I decided to change myself. Of course I didn't do it all alone, but with the help of people who'd already trodden the path of wealth and offered their help generously and gladly! And I hope that I can be one of the people helping you to change if you wish to.

In the last decade of studying, training others and observing their journeys, I discovered four ingredients and proven principles to lasting wealth, which I call the four parts of the "Wealth Diamond." In that time I must have read hundreds of books on wealth myself, attended dozens of courses and seminars and spend hundreds of thousands to develop myself and change my mindset.

I've been asked many times by my students to put my take on things, my unique combination of teachings, derived from my life and my studies, into writing.

You might wonder -- and I asked myself -- if the world indeed needs another book on wealth and money. Well, you can guess by holding a copy of Wealth DNA in your hand I decided it was worth the time and effort, as I believe it has a new take on wealth and what creates it.

Because of my story, which I shared in parts with you, I'm possibly one of the most qualified people to talk about the "gulf" between being broke and desperate to "living the dream." I was almost proud of my poverty and self-negation because it was part of my identity. From my own experience from wanting to be wealthy, people born into wealth or with wealth passed on are sometimes hard to relate to. It's easy for the billionaire to tell you how he made another billion, but how does that help you now? And can they teach?

Since 2006, while changing my fortunes, I have dedicated my life to learning not just how to do it for myself, but also to pass my learnings on to others, aiming to teach and inspire others, too. My passion and desire in writing this book is that I can help you do the same as I did: remove your limitations to wealth fast, despite your past, and create your new, ideal Wealth DNA.

Crossing The Line

There is a concept I call "living above the line." Now if there is an "above the line," there must logically be a "below the line." Let's start there, because this is where I lived for many years and where most people live who don't have what they want.

Everybody manifests. If you want it or not, you got today what you manifested based on your past behaviour. I call it the "wheel of manifestation" (discussed in detail later in the book). Whatever you have and are today is a result and outcome of what you've already done. Nobody would wake up wealthy one day and not know how he or she manifested it.

It's like taking notes on my computer to write this book. I'm putting in effort and then, when I print, I'm creating a version in the physical world. I print from my nice Apple laptop, and they print on nice, thick, textured paper here in Dubai – I manifested that.

The result, the reality, the manifestation – that is what you get. And when you have your result, there is no point blaming or complaining or justifying. I know that nearly everybody in the world would like different results in one area or another. This is why you are reading this book. You want to have more wealth as defined by you.

If you felt perfectly happy, spiritually fulfilled, completely in love with your family, in perfect health and with all the money you ever wanted in the bank, I doubt you'd spend (or invest) time buying or reading a book about Wealth DNA.

Whenever I do a live talk, I ask, "Who in this room would like to lose a pound or two in weight?" Guess what? Literally everybody does. I want to lose some weight! I used to be three stone heavier than I am now, but I'm still thinking, I need to lose some weight. So here's the thing: We set our own standards. The quality of our life is directly related to the standards we hold ourselves to. Standards, that's all it is.

If you're happy to live in a small one bedroom flat, just scrape by and eat spam, then those are standards. And who sets them? You. They are obviously influenced by many other factors like your upbringing, your peer group, and so on (detailed later in "Values"), but somehow you are OK with them. You accept them.

You might have heard people use phrases like, "Man. If it wasn't for BLANK, then I'd be fine!" (or rich or happy). Replace BLANK with pretty much whatever you want: taxes, government, the economy, my education, peer group, my country, pay cheque, salary, wife, husband, kids, health, background, schooling... I mean, the list goes on and on. It's all the same thing. It's blaming circumstances. It's relinquishing responsibility to outside forces and circumstances, which makes you a victim. They are all just stories. Take it from me. I've spun most of these stories for a lot of my life, and they are just Band-Aids – they hide the problem but don't make it go away and they don't really fix the issue. And this is especially common in the area of wealth (or lack of).

I call it "the list of excuses." I mean, they are valid factors that increase or decrease your odds of winning the game of wealth, but they are by no means determining! Here are some of the ones I used that successfully kept me away from wealth. Warning from the department of wealth: These are dangerous delusions and will have a detrimental influence on your financial health.

I'm from Austria. How do you expect me to do well? I was a drug addict from age fourteen to twenty-one. I was twenty years in a religious cult. I have no degree. My dad didn't know how to handle money. I never had money. And the list goes on and on. Well, these are not the best credentials to become wealthy, they are not a great set of Wealth DNA, but that is the whole point – it doesn't matter where you start. You start wherever you are. Where else could you start? And then you set a goal, keep the eyes on the prize and keep at it. Your money blueprint, your Wealth DNA, will change.

So this list of excuses I just shared – I could have used them through all my life. Nobody would have minded it. Actually most people would have given me a pat on the shoulder and said, "I understand." And little would they have known that by showing understanding and being seemingly compassionate they would have contributed to my financial and emotional demise, justifying my poor standards backed up by a bunch of pathetic excuses. We all have a story. And I'm sure that mine is by no means the worst (not that we are in competition). The only thing that matters is, How are you gonna use your story? As a club to beat yourself up with? Or as motivation to get going? It is completely your choice. This book shows you how to back yourself and change. The more you study people who became successful, the more you understand they all have a story they could have used as an excuse to stay poor, but they used it as a reason to become wealthy. Many of them had a low point and turned it all around. Now, you don't have to have had a messed-up youth to become wealthy. It's not really helping, but as a story of proof it's more powerful – as us humans do look for excuses not to do things.

Some people blame what they have or don't have. They blame their assets. That is as if a farmer were to blame the soil and the seed and the sun. Well – that's all he's got to work with. And that's all you got. Your soil is your environment – from family to marketplace. Your seed is your talents and limitations. The sun is the outside support and people around you that help you make it happen.

Stop Blaming What You've Got

There's a great story in a book I'm pretty sure you've heard of. It's been around for a while - an international bestseller with over a billion copies in print. And it doesn't matter if you are Christian or not – there are some great stories in the Bible.

When I heard this story first at school as a twelve- year-old kid I totally misunderstood the teaching. (By the way, is it possible that you might have misunderstood or misinterpreted some truths of life and missed their message?) Today I got it. I had to read it again and again and I needed someone to help me understand its meaning. Here is how I recall the story: A father has three sons. He has to go away for a while and gives his three sons a differing amount of talents. The first one gets one talent, the second one gets five talents, and the third one is given ten talents. Now, a talent was a currency back then, but of course the metaphor is that we are born with a different amount of talents. So anyway, as a kid I'm thinking, Whoa! That's not fair! It's not evenly distributed. How can a father do that? and so on. Well let me break it to you (me), kiddo – life ain't fair. And no amount of redistribution and welfare system is gonna change that. It's just the way it's set up; it's in nature and in our human nature. We're all different. If we distributed all the wealth, what would happen? You got it: It would all redistribute to those who were previously wealthy. We'll discuss later why that is. Back to the story, sorry for interrupting myself.

So the father goes away and wants his sons to do something with the talents he's given them. When he comes back he says, "Okay. Let's tally up. What were you guys up to?"'

He goes to the first son: "So I gave you ten talents. What did you do?" The son says, "I had ten and now I have twenty." Father replies, "Good on you. Well done! You doubled your investment."

He then asks the second son, "How did you get on? What did you do?" Son replies, "You gave me five – now I have ten!" Father is pleased: "Good on you. Well done!"

They are not equal, but they both doubled their father's investment.

So lastly he goes to the kid he gave one talent to. Poor kid – only one talent. But hey, we don't all have the same opportunity and we don't all start from the same place.

So the father asks his son, "What did you do with one talent?" Son replies: "I know you're a tough father so I thought I better keep it safe. So, I buried it and here it is. You can have it back!" Father is not impressed.

So here is what happens next: The father gets upset and takes the one talent and gives it to the son who has twenty! When I heard that first, I couldn't sleep for days! Thought God was a right old meany.

So, why did the father take the one talent away? Because the son didn't do anything with it. Was the kid expected to make twenty out of one? No. Just make two! Use the talent. Do whatever you can. We are never all equal, but you have to apply what you got – the seed, the soil, the sun. What you've been given, you've got to use. That's all that's asked from you.

The book doesn't say that they all pooled their talents together and then shared them equally. And as a matter of fact he didn't give the one talent to the guy who had ten; he gave it to the guy who already had twenty. And that is how money and energy and wealth works. Like attracts like.

So don't blame what you got. Don't blame what you haven't got. Don't blame who didn't give it to you. We all start somewhere. It's a journey. The two thousand-year-old lesson, which is just as relevant today is you have to use what you've got.

So, there are three things people below the line do that keeps them below the line and keeps them from using what they've got to the best of their ability. That keeps them in a state of being a victim. The first one we discussed is blame. Here's the second one: complain. Complaining disempowers you. The third one is justify.

Blame. Complain. Justify. The Evil Dream Stealer Triplets!

Now, we can observe that most people live below the line because you can hear them blame, complain and justify pretty much all day long. And keeping up those stories and excuses takes energy. Valuable energy you can instead invest into changing your Wealth DNA.

Living Above The Line

We discussed what living below the line means and what detrimental effect it has on your wealth and your life in general. So what's above the line?

Just one thing: complete and full responsibility for your actions and your results. Or as I like to write on the flipchart on Wealth Breakthrough Live – response-ability. Because you can change and increase your ability to respond to whatever happens in life and therefore create better results, changing your Wealth DNA.

The good news is that you don't have to be perfect at this stuff. Just get started and then keep going, checking your results along the way. I found that it's actually a relief to take responsibility for your results and exit the blame game.

The universal wheel of manifestation is in place. If you sow the seed with the sun and the soil, something will happen. You do your work and you do your weeding and you look after your crop, and then it's harvest time. And at that point, you're just going to put your hand up and say, "Look. That's what I got." If it's great, congratulations! You earned it. You deserve it. If it's bad, well – you earned it and you deserved it. You deserve whatever you got. If you don't like what you got, tough. Change what you do. In life you don't get what you need, you get what you deserve (or as Bill Gates say, you get what you negotiate). The next year you carry this knowledge forward and you get a better harvest. And each year you get a better harvest. And the odd year it rains too much or not enough, but you carry on and you get more knowledge and experience. Sometimes you can control what happens, and sometimes you can't and you don't get the results you want, but you're always totally responsible for your actions.

Let me give you a practical example from my own situation. I recently agreed to buy a pub for cash and convert it to eighteen rooms and use the surplus land to build more assets or sell it on. Not only will that be a great return on my money invested, it will be an asset with half a million pounds in equity and generate passive income from rent.

I was only able to pull this deal off because I radically improved my response-ability to an opportunity I was offered. Just a couple of years ago there was no way I could have done that.

Without any of the following I wouldn't have been able to see, exploit or manifest this 'opportunity'.

- *the knowledge about types of property investments*
- *the connections, network and partners to be invited*
- *the financial connections to get the money*
- *the confidence to enter the deal*
- *and so on...*

The point is they are all things I can improve upon and influence and can take responsibility for. Now this project was at first waaaay outside my comfort zone, which simply means I haven't done anything on that scale before. But sitting here in the Atlantis in Dubai, which has over 1,500 rooms you gain some perspective of scale. It might be big for me. It might be outside my comfort zone. But then I look around me, I see people doing ten, hundred, thousand times bigger deals than this pub. They do hotels; they do Islands in the shape of palms in the sea! And that has never been done before.

So all I need to understand is this: What I attempt has been done before. It is possible. I can do it too and I will grow as a result of it.

The Wheel Of Life And The Wheel Of Manifestation

Everyone wants different results; some of us in many areas of our life. Others just in a single area. I'm guessing you invested in this book and you are investing in yourself because you want more Wealth. So do I.

When I run my Wealth Breakthrough Live events in the UK, we do an exercise where people evaluate their own life in 8 areas. The basic 8 areas we use are:

Business/Career
Money/Wealth
Personal Growth/Spirituality
Love/Romance

Friends/Family
Fun/Recreation
Health/Vitality
Home & Work Environment

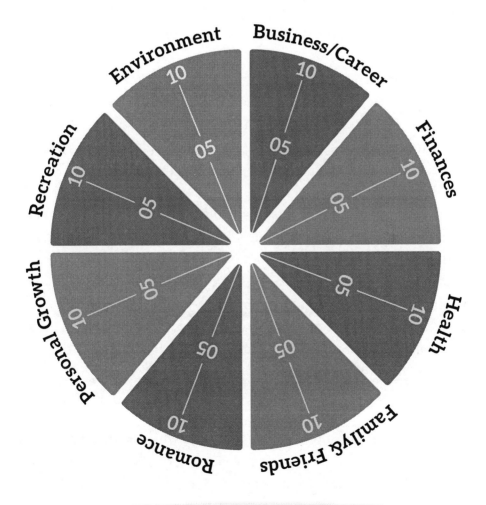

Assign each of the eight areas to a segment of a circle or wheel, and then mark yourself out of 10. There is no wrong or right – but evaluate it based on where youyotuhijnukstyou are from 1-10....

The exercise is called the Wheel of Life, and I've done it at least once a year for the last 10 years since I discovered it. It is a bit like setting your goals and looking back each year, but in a measured, yardstick and visual way, which I like. You will work out that some areas of your life are less perfect than others. You will also notice that once you connect the dots, you will have a shape or an area.

Imagine this being the wheel of the vehicle that takes you through the adventure called life. How smooth a ride would you have? Have you got small wheels (meaning you can't go very fast) or do you have larger wheels? Would the shape of your wheels give a bumpy ride or one that is smooth and balanced?

Another observation is of the area you are covering – the maximum being a complete circle of tens that can give you the ultimate fulfillment. If your area is tiny and oddly shaped, how can you live to your ability? One low area could pull the rest in, and every area affects all the other areas. Whenever you do this exercise you'll find that there are a few areas that are lagging behind. Normally as humans we'd ignore these areas, as we prefer to focus on the things we know how to do well.

The point of this exercise, though, is to identify which areas of your life need the most improvement and also which of the areas will have the most leverage in your life. This normally will improve all other areas, like wealth improving your areas of health and family.

Let's say, for example, that you realise that your health and vitality is at a 5 out of 10, which results in low energy. Would it be fair to assume that your love and romance and your business and career would benefit if you pushed this area to a level 7 out of 10?

What if you realise that your wealth and money area was at a 3? Would you be able to improve every other area of your life if you moved this to a 5 in the next twelve months? Would you be able to be, do and have more of what you love?

Your goal is to achieve higher and higher levels of fulfillment in your life, as you hold yourself to higher and higher standards as you progress up and out in the scale.

Once you know what you want to improve, let's have a look at the wheel of manifestation of how you ended up where you are in the first place and how you can improve your results.

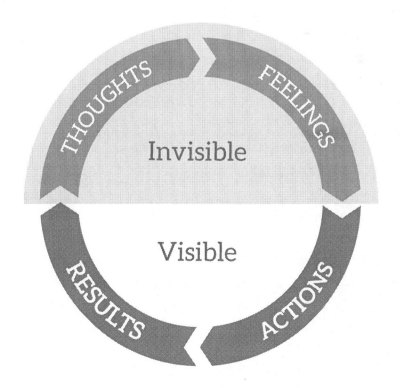

Everybody manifests. You cannot not manifest, just like you cannot not make a decision. Not making a decision is a decision not to do something. It's still a decision. It's the same with manifestation. You cannot choose not to manifest. We all manifest. What I mean by manifest is we bring things into the world that we think about and focus on, whether we like them or not.

Your ideas and desires express themselves in the physical world. Before you roll your eyes and think I'm going all hippie-trippie on you, consider this: What you have right now, what you wear and where you live, who you are with and your state of health -- somehow you brought that upon yourself. Maybe not consciously, but you were part of making this happen. Thoughts become things. Change your thoughts, and your things will change.

So what if you were to become completely conscious not just of the process of manifestation, but of knowing where to make changes to get the new results you want? Imagine that for a minute.

We all want different results. We established that. But what most people don't want to grasp is the invisible side of the wheel of manifestation. We can see people and ourselves acting in the world. Doing stuff. Being busy. That is, of course, the action that produces the results. These are the two components that are visible.

But there are also two components that are invisible, like invisible strings of a puppet that in reality direct your actions and results. One of the two invisible forces that influence your actions are your feelings. How you feel about what you do is paramount. You can do something with a "have-to-succeed" attitude or you can "give it a go" or you can "know that it will fail." Which feeling will have a greater chance of success?

Let me give you a more practical example: Did you ever attempt to lose some weight? Well, the answer for 99 per cent of people is yes.

Have you got references in your life when you wanted to lose weight and succeeded and other times when you wanted to and failed? Again, the answer is yes for most people. If so, what was the difference?

You knew what to do, right? That wasn't the problem. You knew the actions. Everyone knows how to lose weight. Eat less and exercise more. Duh? But when I checked last, there are 98,292 books on losing weight on Amazon. Why do most fail to achieve a very simple and measurable result like losing body weight?

It's because the result is all based on your feelings about doing the required actions. "I have to lose weight by (insert date) and I know this diet will work for me" will be a lot more successful than "I don't think this diet will work for me. None of them ever have. But let's try it anyway. Let's see how it goes." It's obvious. And it's the same in wealth or any other areas of your life.

Feelings or emotions are driven by your thoughts. Every thought has an associated emotion. Most of them were created unconsciously and in your past. So we're screwed? Luckily not! The important point to note is (and science like neuroplasticity has proven) that you can change the linked emotion that is connected to a thought.

If, for example, I mention the word money, you will have a bunch of emotions linked the thought of money. What about cash? The same goes for every single word that has meaning for you. If I mentioned krieg, it most likely wouldn't trigger a lot of feelings for you unless you speak German, but if I told you it is the German word for war, you would surely have a set of emotions for that thought, even if you have no personal experience of it.

It's your thoughts that influence your feelings that drive the actions that create the results. This is the Wheel of Manifestation.

So the wheel of manifestation is turning ... the only question is, *Are you going round in circles, are you on a downward spiral toward a crash or are you onwards and upwards?*

Why Is This Book Called Wealth DNA?

Why call this book Wealth DNA? Good question. I believe every human being wants to be wealthy (even if they don't want to admit it), and recent studies have shown us that DNA can be changed, when everyone thought it had previously been pre-written, or fixed.

"That's just who I am" doesn't stand anymore. If you want to be wealthy, you can be. Regardless of your DNA. Wealth is not in your genes, nor is poverty. You can change it. You can create it. It is not already written, it is not your destiny to be or not to be, it is simply up to you. In this book you'll discover the timeless and proven principles that for generations people have used to build wealth.

What Is Wealth?

Wealth is not just about money. But wealth really is a lot about money. Money magnifies, augments and enriches every aspect of your life; therefore you cannot be truly wealthy without an abundance of money. But you can not be wealthy even if you have a lot of money.

Many people say that wealth is about health, but if you're broke it's hard to properly look after your body. Other people say that your wealth is in your relationships with others, but if you have no money it's certainly harder to develop those relationships or give the gifts both physical and intangible. Other people say that your wealth is in spirituality or philanthropy, but you can't give back what you haven't got. Others think that wealth is all about the money you have, but money alone doesn't make you happy, and without happiness you don't have Wealth. From my observation having been broke for most of my life and having turned it around, money can truly enhance every aspect of your life.

If you're worried that money will change you, it will and it won't. At one of my live events, Wealth Breakthrough Live, I am often challenged that money changes people. It will change you in that it will make you more of what you already are. But it won't change you because all it will do is make you more of what you already are. If you're insecure, you'll spend more money to try and rid yourself of the insecurity. You'll buy more expensive face cream and Botox or cars and toys. If you give everything away, you'll just give more away, making your gifts and donations bigger and more frequent.

So if you're worried money will change you, why don't you go out there and become a multi-millionaire? If you find you don't like who you become, give it all away and go back to being broke. At least then you'll know for sure. Or if you don't like who you become but you want to keep the money, at least you can afford the best celebrity therapist to help get over yourself.

Don't make assumptions about being wealthy, at least until you've tried it. Having negative associations - and we'll talk more about this later in the book - is actually one of the things that will stop you from acquiring and attracting wealth. I can say from experience that money magnifies everything and can make every area of your life more wealthy. But it can also exaggerate what is bad if you don't learn how to manage it properly. If you have a gambling addiction, you think it's going to miraculously get better with more money?

The way I define it, real wealth is having a legacy and purpose, with high levels of health and energy, to develop rich relationships, funded heavily and freely by assets and income. Money is the vehicle that fuels the legacy, health and energy allow us to fulfil it and rich relationships share and expand the legacy and give it meaning, which all in turn create more money. And thus it continues to fulfil itself. Who wouldn't want that? This is why I confidently proclaim that I believe everyone wants to be wealthy.

In this definition, wealth is broken down into five categories: legacy, purpose, relationships, health and energy and financial freedom. The Wealth Pentagon shows that they are all interconnected and feed each other. You cannot have wealth in my definition unless you have all five points of the **Wealth Pentagon.**

The Wealth Pentagon
Wealth DNA

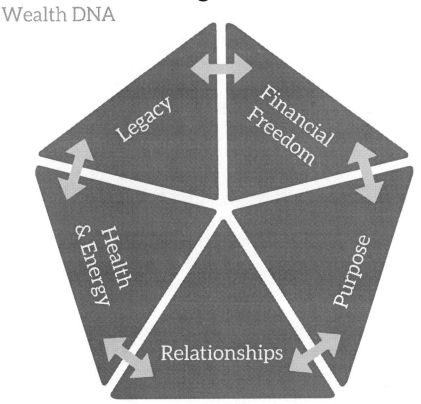

Legacy

Legacy answers the question. 'Did you matter?'

Legacy is the memory of you. It is what's left of you after you are gone. It is the difference you made while you were here and how you helped develop mankind. It is your "dent in the universe." Without legacy you were nothing but worm food (apologies for the bleak image if you are a visual person). Without legacy you have no purpose to fulfil and you have no direction in life. You float down someone else's stream blown by someone else's wind. Legacy is your epitaph. Legacy is your torch carried by others from your funeral and how long it lasts afterwards. Legacy drives you and gets you through the dark days of life's winters.

Purpose

Your purpose is how you deliver and fulfil your legacy.

For most of my life I struggled with "Why am I here?" and "What am I supposed to do?" questions. Not only did I meditate on the question for almost twenty years without a definitive answer, I did many courses on having direction in life, discovering meaning and purpose and finding my true calling. The reality is that most of what I finally found out I already knew. It just seemed too easy and too simple. I was just afraid to get on with it and was looking for some kind of permission from someone else. In the end you know when you know! You know when you're in flow.

Many people in the personal development industry spend long weekends to convince people they should create a business around doing what they love. I personally believe that this is in most cases bad advice, as many things people might enjoy are not easy to monetise.

My suggestion is different. Choose an already proven wealth vehicle and then use the money you make to do what you love! If you can make it coincide, then good for you; that is a nice bonus. But if I had the choice between struggling artistically making money out of my average songwriting capabilities in an unpredictable and fickle music industry or using proven wealth models to make vast sums of money and have time and freedom through passive income to play the guitar and sing when I choose for fun, I'd do the latter. No competition. Obviously (and that is one of the reasons many people choose the first and end up being broke and losing their passion) the second path takes a bit of time and pleasure-delaying, but it will serve you better in the long term.

Having purpose for a human being comes primarily from being productive and needed in some way. The real enemy is boredom and survival stress. I feel it is very important to spend some time to consider those questions: "Why am I here?" and "What am I supposed to do?" Because too many people are floating in a hypnotised coma not knowing why they are doing what they are doing but knowing that they hate it. But then get on with it and make it happen. There is really no point in spending years talking about it and philosophising about what could be. Start the process and see if you like where it leads you. If you don't, change. You're not a tree.

To have the feeling of purpose, meaning or even fulfilment, you have to keep growing and expanding. Human beings, like every living thing on this planet, have to evolve. And to discover new things is exciting and at times a bit intimidating. Many people settle into the illusion of security of a job, which will not allow them to reach the next level of income and ultimately the wealth they desire.

But the life of more fulfilment and the next level of income is right outside their current comfort zone. What I find fascinating is that the moment you have expanded your comfort zone, it becomes your new comfort zone.

I also find it fascinating that many wealthy people are compelled to give back and help others. It's part of who we are as human beings. And it gives purpose and meaning to the giver. And if you have a cause you're passionate about, would $100 million help that cause? And so our purpose, to fulfil our legacy, is always greater than ourselves. It has to be for us to grow and expand.

Relationships

Your relationships are the conduits and interconnections to deliver, expand and spread your legacy. No one on the planet can survive alone, and wealth cannot be created in isolation. No one is totally independent, and in fact the poorest people in the world are not just the most dependent (babies, slaves) but also independent (meaning, in that context, not connected). Wealth comes from interdependence, from a world-wide interconnected relationship network through which your legacy, purpose and goodwill spread like wildfire. So as much as our aim for freedom means independence, fulfilment through relationships comes from interdependence.

There are four areas of relationships you need to cultivate in your life that create wealth: your relationship with yourself, your relationship with your friends and family, your business relationships (suppliers, customers, staff, peers) and your relationship with your wider community (all the way to your environment and the world as a whole). The size and quality of these four areas of relationships, woven in with the five categories of the Wealth Pentagon, will dictate and represent your level of wealth.

Health & Energy

Your goal in health and energy should be to live for a hundred years with passion and enthusiasm. Without energy you will have no motivation to live your legacy. Health is wealth because the longer you live the longer you have to fulfil your purpose and leave a lasting legacy.

Warren Buffett, one of the richest men the world has ever seen and perennially in the top five of the richest people in the world, remarks that one of the major reasons for his wealth is that he's been doing it longer than everyone else. Eight decades dedicated to wealth. (He would never have gotten on the Rich Lists had he started at thirty-one and died at thirty-seven of a drug overdose.)

They say that if you don't have your health, you have nothing. And it is true! Everything pales into insignificance when you're not healthy. It preoccupies your mind, it preoccupies your body. It stops you from doing what you should be doing. I know - I have been unwell for quite a few years of my life. And it sucked. It was never very serious, and I'm always inspired to read about and see people who have overcome real health issues and life-threatening diseases. But I was sick enough to worry about it all day long, and it impacted everything I did.

When you are of ill health, all you can focus your time and energy on is getting better. And so you fall behind in every other area of your life. It is vital to maintain and improve your health while you are living your legacy through purpose, so that you can have the time and energy to do it. Ill health, or dis-ease of the mind and body, is something that we can influence until death comes near.

Doctors now agree that stress is a major contributing factor in every disease. The fact that I had serious reflux and was about to have a stomach operation simply meant I couldn't "digest" my life anymore. I couldn't swallow it anymore. My body kept reminding me that I had to make a change. Or multiple changes, as it were. My environment was not that good for me. So if you want to live until you're 100 (and science tells us that this is easily possible), there are some things that you can do to facilitate this. You see, wealthy people live longer. It's not just the money. It's having a great environment (the place you live and hang out and the people you live with and hang out with), having an exciting life and purpose, having access to the best nutrition and, if necessary, the best healthcare. Having gratitude and happiness has also been proven to prolong life, and recent research suggests that having a purpose will keep your heart beating a lot longer.

When I was broke I just didn't have (or make) the time to look after myself. These days I'm almost obsessed with health and energy. I know that everything worth doing requires energy, from being onstage to writing this book, from spending quality time with my wife and kids to building a business. If it needs doing, it needs energy. And that's on a good day. What if you're facing obstacles and challenges? It's good to be full of beans.

So if you don't have the time and money to look after your health and energy, push that right up your priority list. Or your list of values, as you will discover later. Because of all the assets we'll need and want to be wealthy, this one's non-negotiable. The way I see it, either you choose to look after your health while you have a choice or you will be forced to look after it when you're ill.

Financial Freedom
My definition of financial freedom is *'your desired lifestyle funded from passive income from assets.'* It is the monetary system that'll

fund your purpose and fuel your legacy, which is delivered to the world through your relationship interdependence. Got that? Great.

Without assets (brand, legacy, property, IP, licenses, stocks and shares, businesses, e-commerce) you have to exchange time for money. That time exchange is likely to take you away from your legacy and purpose, therefore dwindling your wealth despite paying the bills. This never-ending cycle of keeping your head just above water leaves no time to make a lasting difference. And even while you think you're staying afloat, you're actually sinking slowly as valuable time ticks by that you could use to build passive income streams to fund your dream lifestyle.

Through this book you will learn that you might be able to match your purpose and passion with your profession, or more likely invest in assets that will pay you so that you have more free time to pursue whatever you want.

What Is DNA And Why It's Good News For You

When the 1962 Nobel Prize in Physiology was awarded jointly to Francis Harry Compton Crick, James Dewey Watson and Maurice Hugh Frederick Wilkins "for their discoveries concerning the molecular structure of nucleic acids and its significance for information transfer in living material," it was also concluded that DNA was fixed. Today's science community has changed its tune: "DNA is dynamic and has high energy; not stiff or static as first envisioned," reads a report out of the Baylor College of Medicine.

And there are so many parallels with our perceptions of what is born and what is learned, what is nature and what is nurture, that the Wealth DNA concept was born – the hybrid of nature and nurture and the myth of fixed "talent," DNA.

So although deoxyribonucleic acid (DNA) is, according to the Oxford English Dictionary, "a self-replicating material present in nearly all living organisms as the main constituent of chromosomes" and "the carrier of genetic information," it actually, amazingly to scientists, responds to the environment you're in. If you believe that you are at the mercy of your genetic code, then here's great news: You're not.

According to Carolanne Wright at NaturalNews.com, "According to the science of epigenetics (the study of how environmental factors outside of DNA influence changes in gene expression), stem cells and even DNA can be altered through magnetic fields, heart coherence, positive mental states and intention." You might be struggling to influence your magnetic field or heart coherence, but here is the good news: We can all influence our mental states and intention, and not just in a specific situation but in our physical makeup. We can change and improve our own human code. I find this fascinating and truly amazing, and top modern scientists around the world now agree: Genetic determinism is a flawed theory.

So calling this book Wealth DNA honors the fact that although you are in large parts what you've been handed through your genes, new discoveries clearly state you can't use that as an excuse any longer. You have a say. So use that power. Wealth DNA will show you what you can do.

For the purpose of this book I want to propose the theory that wealth has its own DNA, has its own building blocks - and in this book I have decoded it for you. The secret of wealth. Wealth DNA - the proven principles of lasting wealth. A code that you can crack and master to create lasting wealth.

Why You Should Care About Neuroplasticity

According to Wikipedia.org, "Science tells us this is the process in which your brain's neural synapses and pathways are altered as an effect of environmental, behavioural and neural changes." When it comes to neuroplasticity, the brain is a lot like film.

According to Sarah Cobarrubias at education-portal.com, "When you photograph a picture of, say, a mountain, you're exposing the film to new information - it reacts to the light, and its makeup changes in order to record the image of that mountain. In the same way, your brain's makeup changes when it's exposed to new information so that it may retain that information."

Infinite amounts of neural pathways are created through every thought process, and over time they become habits, memories, reactions, emotions, instincts and intuition. You have the power to consciously create these neural pathways, which to victims are subconscious disempowering habits they are slaves to, and therefore write your own positive actions and behaviours that become set habits in your brain that then fire on auto-pilot. Just like you subconsciously bite your nails or have cravings, you can subconsciously attract and create wealth.

The Myth Of Talent

Running live workshops and seminars, I get up close and personal with people. I could spend hours after an event talking to people. And I love it. Because of all the people I meet, I'd be an idiot not to spot the common beliefs and thought patterns of people and their relationship to wealth. One of the most common myths is requiring natural ability or talent to be wealthy -- or natural ability to do or be anything, for that matter.

Many times I get compliments from people regarding my ability to manage a room or public speaking, telling me that I have a "natural gift." I normally thank them for the feedback but then point out that the reality is that I have worked on the craft for almost ten years now. I'm glad I got quite good at it - you would kind of expect that, right? This is one of the most common yet most expensive myths, because no one is natural at anything. No one popped out of their mum and, whilst tugging on the umbilical chord, read a balance sheet and was a natural born master of wealth.

Your Wealth DNA has not been formed at birth. You have very few neural pathways set. You are pure potential at birth, but pure potential only. You are nothing and everything. You can be anything with the right upbringing, training, parenting, environment, culture, society, and that anything could be a great guitarist, golfer, tech- head, anything. But there is no special genetic code for guitarist or golfer. Tiger Woods didn't pop out of the womb and boom a 300-yard drive.

Yet you hear it everywhere all the time. "This person has natural talent." "That person was born with a gift." People put others on pedestals who seem to be so "natural" at something, and de-pedestalise others (including themselves) when they feel they can't be, do or have what they want. If you take the time to study the facts, and to study anyone who is successful at anything, you will see that they learned the system, were in the right environment at the right time (either through chance or self creation), and most likely studied or have been trained by the very best in the given field. Sports is a great area to study this. As much as you need some prerequisites to get in the game, getting good or being the best at it has very little to do with talent. Reading Malcolm Gladwell's Outliers or Matthew Syed's Bounce highlights that in a dramatic and hard to believe fashion. So engrained is the myth of talent that we argue in our head with the science.

It is exactly the same on the subject of wealth. And as an example of proof that wealth is not in your DNA, let's look at people who have been given lots of money and see how they used it and dealt with it using their natural ability. I am talking about lottery winners. How many stories have you heard of people winning the lottery and then investing it for a long-term compounded return, building sustainable businesses and creating industry-leading compounded yearly growth to get on the rich list ten years after the windfall? That would be none, right? Why? Because they have no idea how to manage money; they have not changed their Wealth DNA, and if you give someone more money, they will manage it how they have always managed it. It will simply exaggerate what they have always done. Let's look at some real world examples.

Callie Rogers won £1.9m at 16 years old and at age 26 has less than £2,000 of it left. Lisa Arcand won over £1m and was broke after a few years giving it away to friends and spending it on holidays. Lou Eisenberg won $5m in 1981 and now earns just $250 a week from his pension and lives on a trailer park. Robert and Lara Griffith won £2m, blew it on handbags, cars and cosmetics and now have £7 to their combined names. Michael Carrol won £10m at 19 and spent it on drugs, jewellery, parties and cars (and wasted the rest as the joke goes) and now earns £200 a week working in a biscuit factory in Scotland.

So money itself is not the answer - if you want to change your Wealth DNA, you need to work on your skills, knowledge, experience, mindset, network, geography/environment and access to mentors. You will not make more money until you learn to manage what you already have, but the good news is that even if you are £200,000 in credit card debt and you are living at 150 per cent expenditure vs. income, you can learn to start creating more wealth.

Another common belief I hear is that you need money to make money. And therefore it is easy for those who inherit or are born into wealth but not easy for those who don't have any. Sounds like another excuse to me. Remember blame, complain, justify? You might be pleased you didn't inherit wealth, as studies show that just as with lottery wins, second-generation inherited wealth often gets squandered (unless the heirs and heiresses have developed their Wealth DNA).

So you don't need money to make money. If you study the wealthy you will see that this is a myth. 2nd generation Wealth is often squandered because the recipient (children of wealthy parents) doesn't know how to manage it properly. In fact statistically, 60% of inherited businesses are lost by future generations. A second generation business has only a 53% chance of surviving another ten years, despite it surviving and thriving through a generation, and a third generations business less than 32%. (According to the IFOB). You see they didn't learn what it took to create Wealth, so they often don't value it; they haven't created the right DNA. It's not that they can't, it's just that they haven't learnt it (yet). This is the same in business, where 2nd generation management often mismanage the business because they didn't create the DNA that learned how to build and manage it. They don't know what they don't know. If it was born into their DNA, then they would be able to do it from birth, but that is ridiculous.

I have read many, many autobiographies of the super rich and am fortunate enough to have many wealthy friends, and nearly all of them are self-made. There are 625,000 self-made millionaires in the UK alone. And of all millionaires in the UK, 76 per cent are self-made. Once I finally turned a corner in my life and knew I could change my Wealth DNA, I made it my life's mission to learn from the money masters. Everything that the poor think they know about Lord Sugar or the Dragons or Donald Trump, based on what they see on TV, is almost all wrong. I know because I have met many of them or because my good friends have.

Almost none of them were born into wealth. In fact, many were born with no inheritance and created all their wealth themselves. Many were poor and rebellious at school, many had challenging upbringings, but all created their own Wealth DNA. They are all "normal" people like you and me, no Super DNA, no silver spoon or divine right or authority.

So now that I have told you that Wealth is neither part of your birth's DNA and that you should be lucky no to be given millions before you learned how to manage and that you should be grateful that you haven't inherited Wealth (let's tick then off our 'If I just ...' list) you might want to know what actually does create your reality. From success to money to the combination of it all, true Wealth. Well I'm glad you asked.

Here are the distilled six main influencing factors and ingredients to help you create your own Wealth DNA. I haven't made them up, they are proven to be the most important reasons for your results.

1. Knowledge
2. Experience
3. Network
4. Mentors
5. Environment
6. Parents

Knowledge

Pretty much anything can be learned, as long as it is physically or humanly possible. Yet even the boundaries of the humanly possible are being stretched by mankind. Think flight, space exploration, cloning. Study the authors, trainers, mentors and real life masters of wealth. With the Internet, fibre optics and social media, this is easier than ever and at your fingertips at the speed of light. Follow the trail they have blazed and leverage their mistakes. Don't reinvent the wheel. Use mentors and trainers to guide you through the shortcuts and avoid the expensive and time-consuming pitfalls. Be an eager student to those who've spent decades practicing and mastering their art, and get all their experience condensed into hours or days. The investment you make in your knowledge is the best investment that pays the most interest, so invest in yourself generously.

Experience

All the knowledge in the library doesn't get results, and as one of my mentors once remarked: 'to know and not to do is not to know'. Go out there and test what you learn. If you're scared, start small. If it's property you want to have a go at, buy a one bed flat as your first property investment, not the Atlantis hotel in Dubai that I am currently sat in writing this, which has 23 floors, 1,539 rooms, 22 restaurants, and is worth around $500,000,000 US dollars according to Wikipedia. Whatever you are putting off or you fear doing is the very thing you probably need to do now. Whatever you learn will be slightly different in your personal experience when you implement it, no matter how good the trainer, author or mentor is. So put your knowledge into practice, and work out that final 5% that makes it work in your own world. Leverage 95% of their mistakes and create your own special flavour of personal Wealth DNA. The most expensive mistake is the one never made.

Network

According to John C. Maxwell, "Your network is your net-worth." Your ability to solve problems, access deep pockets and build the best team is directly linked to the black book of personal contacts you have on speed dial. Your biggest problem is no problem for someone else. And if they're on your speed dial or someone in your network can introduce them to you, your biggest problem is not a problem anymore.

Here is a tip: Invest at least a third of your work time in your network, take it as seriously as sales in your business and see the people in your network as you would your favourite collection. Some people boast about their collection of shoes or watches; you could reel off a who's who in your network. The secret wealthy people know is the wealthy people they know.

Mentors

You wouldn't get in a Helicopter and on the first lesson kick out the instructor and give it a fly yourself. You wouldn't jump out of an Aircraft without an instructor briefing or tandem parachutist. Yet when it comes to Wealth, most people are trying it all on their own. And then they're surprised they crash and burn. That's crazy!

Find and cherry pick those who are wealthy, in many different businesses and niches, and stick close to them. Some you can hire to be your personal mentor or part of a mentorship group, and this investment will pay a huge return. Paid mentors are committed not only to physically show you (which you can't get from a book), but also to keep you accountable, which is the missing piece for most people. In most cases the rule is simple: Get the best mentor you can afford. In most cases the more you pay, the better mentor you get and the better and faster your results.

You can also get "free" mentors, who just eat the food at the expensive restaurants you take them to and chat about what they do. If you get a chance, offer to pay the bill, let the wine flow and hang off their every word and you will grow (and maybe get drunk in the process).

Environment

There are at least two types of environment. You and your immediate environment like the apartment or house you live in and your immediate family. And then there is your wider environment. If you wanted to build a technology business, for example, it would be smart to locate yourself in Silicon Valley. If you wanted to be an artist, setting up in London or New York or Paris would make sense. Some people have the added fortune that they were born or located in the right place at the right time, so that they had easy access to facilities, technology and whatever tools and equipment helped develop the skills to be great at something. There are exceptions, of course, like Elon Musk, who started the electric car company Tesla in California – but then again he is a trailblazer and billionaire maverick.

Bill Gates, Steve Jobs, Steve Wozniak and other big names in tech were all located in the same geographic area through the 80's where the most advanced (and rare) super computers the size of buildings were located. This was fortunate for them at the time.

Many of the best UK golfers have relocated to Florida to be around the best golfers, coaches and facilities. And at one point British and Irish golfers virtually owned the top 10, using the location that the previous best were born in to accelerate their way up the world's best list.

You can either be a victim to the wrong environment or you can change it and set yourself up for success. Where do many wealthy people frequent? Can you spend more time there? What facilities do they have access to? It might not sound quite as glamorous as moving to Florida, but I recently moved to Peterborough to change my environment. I'm working closely with Rob Moore and his companies, and it just made sense to live there for the next chapter of my life.

The culture and media of your environment will vary. To exaggerate the point, for example, a communist country is not conducive to free market enterprise. You cannot escape your environment. You are invisibly entangled in it. That's one of the reasons I love to travel, as I'm always blown away to see how my environment changes my perception of what is possible and how I feel. For example, Dubai – it's impossible not to be inspired and impressed by what human vision and ingenuity has achieved there in such a short time.

Choose what you read and watch and protect yourself from messages that don't suit your legacy and purpose. With the Internet, audio books and social media, you have more control and more choice over what you feed your brain, and therefore mass media can indoctrinate you less. If you commuted to London every day on the tube (I do remember those days but do not miss them) you'd see literally every single person read the same free paper (the metro) and taint their minds with random stories and irrelevant information. I say irrelevant in the context of necessity to make decisions that very day. And guess what? They'll talk about this garbage at the water cooler later that day. If you think about it, a newspaper pays journalists to scour the world to collect the worst things that happened (called news) and then collate them for you to freak yourself out. Check out, by the way, what happens to your ability to use your human intelligence if you are in a state of fear and panic. Do that every day and you will impede your ability to create wealth.

You can watch Bloomberg, listen to business and finance podcasts and watch YouTube channels of your mentors and fill your brain with knowledge regardless of your geographic location, as long as you have Internet access. That is amazing, and most of it inexpensive or free. This is why there are people now out there arguing that Maslow's hierarchy of needs should include WiFi at the base! In the past we didn't have as much control over the factors in this section as we do now. We were born where we were born, and much of our geography was down to luck. Now you have full control and can be anywhere in the world at the speed of fibre optic.

Parents

Your parents are likely to be your biggest influence in who you have become (unless you were sent away to a boarding school run by a religious cult from the age of three). They will have raised you as best they can with the tools and resources they had. But they may not have the right resources to help develop your Wealth DNA. Or, as I will share in a story of an unconscious money belief, they might even pass on some real obstacles to your ability to create Wealth. It's never too late though to have a happy childhood, so however old you are and however you were raised, you can go back in your mind, accept and love how you were raised, forgive your parents for what you held against them, and realise that there was benefit in how they raised you that can now form your Wealth DNA the way you wished it was in the first place. Even if they gave you the ultimate 'How NOT to be rich' guide!

If the impression your parents had on you is in the past, then let go of all the poverty messages you are holding, like "Money doesn't grow on trees" or "You have to work hard to make a living." "You get nothing for free in this life" or one of my dad's favourites, "They all have it in for me and want to make it hard for me – but I will work hard." That was all they knew, but if they weren't wealthy then they had poor programming themselves. Check out your family history to understand why if you are interested. There is always a reason. Then accept they did the best they could and let go. Carry forward the good things they did and leave the rest behind and aim to do a better job with your kids if you can.

If you are still under your parents' influence, then take the learnings they give you and work out how this can develop your Wealth DNA. If you feel audacious, try changing your parents' Wealth DNA. My tip would be to change your own results first and see if they want to know what happened.

Let go of any limiting beliefs or false evidence towards wealth and it being some kind of talent, gift or DNA inheritance. It isn't; it is a learned system, and you can learn it, too, like I did and still do. It took me many slow years to get off the ground, but I hope I and this book can help you do it a little quicker.

Why You Need To Be Wealthy

There are many reasons why you should become wealthy. As a matter of fact one of the things my first wealth coach asked me to do when I was still broke was to write down 100 reasons why I HAD to be wealthy. Guess what? I struggled. My mind went blank. Because all I had in my mind were justifications for being broke and why money was bad; I had at least 100 reasons why it was OK not to do well or to be wealthy. But once I got going I found more and more reasons why being wealthy would be a good thing. I didn't get to 100 at first, but it gets easier with time. Try it, it'll be fun! If you feel like you want to do this now, go ahead. But if you don't - don't worry. I hate those books when they say, Do it now - don't carry on unless you've done this and that. And of course, I never do it there and then, and then I feel bad! You know what I mean? So if you want to, write down some reasons why you need to be wealthy. If you can't be bothered, read some of mine...

Here are three of my top reasons why I believe I MUST become and stay wealthy. Not a nice to have, a HAVE to have:

The Wealthy Live Longer And Healthier

Well - being alive is pretty much a prerequisite for the human experience, so having more time on the planet should generally be something you aim for. A shocking recent study has again shown that people with money live a great deal longer than their poorer fellow men...

In Newcastle in North England, the difference in life expectancy between the rich and poor was almost thirteen whopping years! And they don't just live longer -- they are healthier while they live longer. Similar studies in Glasgow and London have confirmed the simple fact

– Wealth and money buys you time! Wealth and money buy you more time to generate more money and more Wealth! Cool.

Now of course it's not the money in itself, but the lifestyle money can afford you. And make no mistake, the future, whatever it may turn out to be, will be expensive! So from better nutrition to better (often private) healthcare, life extension technologies currently reserved for Hollywood celebrities, having less survival stress and a more balanced life, I think money is one of the most important ingredients to a long and happy life.

I don't even want to go down the doom and gloom predictions about your pension pot (or the lack of a pension pot, as it were); just pick up one of the tabloids and you can fill yourself full of the doom. But forget the media hype -- get the facts, and you can see that pensions are worth less, people are living longer and the age you can get hold of your pension is being pushed out and will continue to be pushed out. As I jokingly say onstage, it's now 137! You could demonstrate on the streets, as in France recently, but if there is no money, you can't get your pension. They are printing money as fast as they can (creating inflation and devaluing currency and your savings and pension pot), but it's still not enough to pay for the aging baby boomers' retirement. You might be hanging around this planet for a good few years, so take control of your own pension, now. Draw it when you want, at whatever age you want, or take it all. But make sure you have choice and are not waiting for handouts. Maybe one day in the near future one of our dear politicians will be courageous enough to tell the truth and announce, "This pension thing – we have some bad news, folks..."

The Rising Cost Of Living Expenses And Future Lifestyle

Being here in Dubai definitely puts things into perspective. There is a lot of money here, and there is always another level. But the higher you go, the more space between you and the street if you know what I mean. There are layers of protection. The best way to protect yourself from high inflation, ever-increasing living costs and the ever-growing gap between the rich and the poor is to become rich! And Dubai proves that money attracts money. I sat on the square outside Dubai Mall next to Burj Khalifa (the highest building in the world) amongst thousands of people from around the world. Just ten short years ago it was a building site. No one was there.

Life becomes far simpler when you don't have to look at the price tag of things. Things become faster, more accessible, more convenient and more enjoyable the more affordability you have. I recently noticed that as my earning power has increased as part of my changed Wealth DNA, life seems to have gotten cheaper. Well, that isn't true in an absolute sense, but it sure is true in a relative sense. There is a chapter in this book called the "10x Challenge," which I do an exercise on at Wealth Breakthrough Live. Let's say you are currently earning £100,000 a year and have a comfortable life. How would your life be different if you earned 10 times that, meaning £1 million a year? Would daily life suddenly appear cheaper? Of course it would. I remember driving for miles to save 1p on petrol. It's been a while since I checked or have been worried by the news of petrol prices going up.

But the bad news for the poor is that it is getting harder and harder just to survive. High inflation and increased niching and competition is pushing prices of general and essential items up. The news tell us (it might be true) that there is a "cost of living" crisis and it'll be one of the big topics in the next election in the UK. The best way to combat any of this is to push your wealth up faster and higher to protect yourself and your family. Don't wait for it.

The Connection Between Wealth And Happiness

I know for certain that part of my unhappy years with my first wife were directly linked to having no money and being constantly broke! Money is indeed named one of the primary reasons for the collapse of marriages and other long-term relationships, and I have personal experience as to why. And although they say that money and love have nothing to do with each other, even love can be eroded if the pressures of money keep undermining the self-respect and ability to enjoy life.

Many studies have shown that at a certain level, money and happiness are not connected or related anymore, which simply means you have to create Wealth to be fulfilled and not just accumulate money, but the same study also shows a strong correlation between money and happiness when it comes to the lower levels of income. It's simply really, if you are (or feeling you are) struggling to survive you can't be happy. Check out Maslow's hierarchy of needs, if your main concern and majority of waking hours is consumed by providing food and shelter, you have no time to create meaningful relationships and focus on self-actualisation.

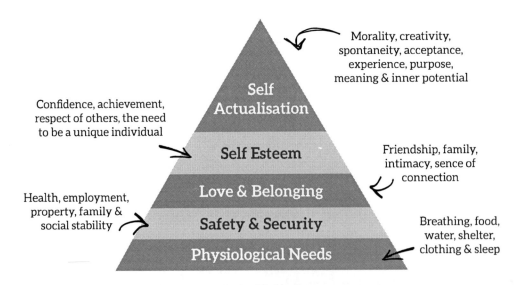

From my own experience I can only testify that I felt stressed, angry, embarrassed and trapped with a distinct lack of choice and freedom when I was fighting to stay afloat. I couldn't treat my wife to any of the finer things in life (which I secretly desired but didn't admit to), I had to work harder and longer to make the same money each year, and that pushed us apart. I could hardly give her and the kids what they needed, so their quality of life diminished, and then either she blamed me or I felt guilt and shame that she would be blaming me - either way it led to the same outcome. And that would in turn cause arguments and truth-withholding, and the embarrassment and shame would manifest in blame and anger, creating more of the same and driving a wedge between us. I wonder how different it would have been had I had wealth back then. No regrets for sure, but to say money and happiness are not connected is quite frankly bollocks! Sorry, but that is my experience.

And it's also weird how different life is on the other side of bad debt. I remember flying back from Ireland in 2010 and a guy at Dublin airport offering me a credit card. You know - some 0 per cent promotion for balance transfers and so on. I had just cleared my debts of over 15 years and for the first time I had money in all my accounts. He stopped me and asked me if I was interested in paying less interest on my debt or if I was looking to consolidate my other debt. When I told him I had none he stared at me in disbelief, as if he'd seen an alien. And I know how he must have felt, because only a few years prior I didn't know a single person who had money. All the people I hung out with were broke and were in debt, too, juggling credit cards. "Good for you, mate!" he said, and I felt great. The problem with bad debt (living beyond your means and spending money on liabilities and debt) is that you are selling off your future! Which in turn limits your choices and infringes on your freedom today, in your day to day existence called life.

What Is Money?

In order to master money, we need to understand money. Most people have never given any thought to what it really is, but we all have heaps of strong emotions and our own meaning attached to it. Positive and negative!

Paper money (notes) isn't anything other than a derivative of cotton (or plastic in some countries) that has virtually no capital value, certainly far less than it promises to be worth. It is a promissory note to pay the bearer and was previously backed by a physical asset as collateral (such as gold in the banks). In effect it is debt created by the banking system. We'll talk about collateral later in the book.

Money has only been the recognised medium of exchange for a brief part of history. Before money, precious metals were used to exchange value, but the flaws in precious metals were the inability to give change and alchemists adding base metals to precious metals to devalue the coin and make their precious metals apparently worth more. This created inflation, the devaluation of money, where it became worth relatively less each year. (Sounds a lot like today's quantitative easing strategy of our new alchemists at the Bank of England.)

Before universal or recognised media of exchange, goods and services were traded. The flaws in this were that it was also difficult to give change, and liquidity (flow that encourages exchange) was low because you could only offer the skill or trade you had as payment (cobbler, butcher) and your customer could only pay with the skill or trade they had (one pair of shoes for one leg of the cow). You get the picture.

I recommend a book called '*The Ascent of Money,*' if you want the full history, I will stick to a brief overview of what's relevant for this book.

So money is simply an evolved, recognised medium of exchanging or trading goods, services or value. If you exchange currency, you expect the same (fair exchange) or higher value (bargain) in return for your money. If you get less, you feel ripped off. Currency enables us to universally quantify, exchange and trade value.

At the time of writing money evolves again. Apple Pay has just hit the news and is being rolled out in the US and across the world, and this new form of cashless exchange is just another evolution of money.

Money actually has no meaning on its own other than its physical form. It is not good, it is not bad. It is not biased other than flowing to those who know how to manipulate the flow of money. Currency literally means "flow," and for the monetary system to work, money must continue to flow.

I play a simple but profound wealth game at Wealth Breakthrough Live called "pass the money." You would get some money and simply pass it around the group. You pass it fast and slow, with no other rules, until you are instructed to stop. I won't ruin the game for you, as I am sure you will play it when we meet; the lessons are quite amazing. But if everyone who was asked to pass the money simply stopped or hoarded or just stuffed the cash into their pockets, the game would stop in three seconds flat. The flow would stop, and so would the exchange.

Money in the world works the same way. You can't save or hoard your way to Wealth. If everyone tried that, money wouldn't flow. You couldn't sell your products or services, people couldn't buy your products or services, and in order to survive we would have to loot and fight and go back to exchanging our skill or 'trade,' for someone else's cow. That is in essence what the whole economy is based on.

Encouraging the flow of money. And the banks and governments try to influence and control where the money flows with interest rates on saving and lending. (A less than perfect system as we can observe).

Here is some ways how you can manipulate the flow of money to attract more in your life:

No Meaning - Your Meaning

Remember money has no meaning. It isn't good or bad, the root of all evil or the answer to all your problems. Money will only make you more of what you already are. If you want to change the amount of money you have in your favour, you need to change you. You give it meaning when you borrow it, while you hold it, while you are the bearer. You never own it, so let go of ownership control of money. You gain some, you spend some, you win some, you lose some. You can get it back and more, and no matter how much money you control in any given period of time, in time it will flow to someone else and to someone else and to someone else.

If you count all the money you have attracted in your life up to now, it's probably quite a lot. You know you can do it; you just need to do it more and quicker and more efficiently and more effectively. The same with how much you've spent, right? The only difference with people who have more is they have attracted more and they have spent more. They have allowed more to flow through their lives. Money was never yours; it's not owed to you, and you don't have to chase it back; just let it flow through you. Attract freely and spend freely, and more will flow through you.

If you gave a philanthropist £20, they would use it to help others, correct? And if you gave a drug addict £20, they would use it to feed their habit (or roll it up to feed their habit), correct? People use money according to their values and beliefs, so look at changing you, as is already happening through reading this book, and you change what money is to you and how much you attract.

More money will come your way when you learn to manage what you already have. Change your meaning; change your physical amount. Change "money doesn't grow on trees" to "there is unlimited money in the universe." Change "you have to work hard for money" to "make your money work hard for you." Change "I don't deserve money" to "I deserve abundant wealth, and it is my right and I will do good with it." Change "money will change me in a bad way" to "money will make me a better person who can serve others better."

Fair Exchange

Flow works best under fair exchange. If you take more money than the value you give, someone will feel ripped off, they will tell others and the flow of money to you (from others, where all money comes from) will dry up. But on the flip side, if you give far too much value and don't charge enough for it, you will become known for it, devalue your products, services and self-worth and people will use you. You will feel constantly taken advantage of and develop a feeling of being exploited, and you might end up hating your customers for paying you too little, which will stop the flow of money.

Currency long-term works best under fair exchange of value, where equal monetary reward is exchanged for value where both parties feel service and gratitude. This then augments in the form of recommendations and repeat business, increases your self-worth (which in turn increases your fees) and attracts the right, higher quality customers. It's well known in business that the acquisition of a new customer is many times more expensive and harder than selling to an existing (happy) customer. So even in simple business terms it makes sense. The big players in retail spend more and more marketing dollars in retaining existing customers through incentives and loyalty programs. There is a reason.

According to Warren Buffet, "Price is what you pay but value is what you get." If you want to dramatically increase your fees, invoices or salary, you need to be able to offer more value first. You have to start the process, because money won't flow to you in the hope or expectation that you will offer the value afterwards. That is called debt.

If you want a salary raise, offer the value and do the work of someone who is paid double, and you will get paid double. And if your current employer won't, go somewhere else where they see and appreciate your value. If it's obvious, you'll get headhunted. If you want customers who pay higher fees, you have to charge higher fees.

It is far easier to discount high fees than it is to double low ones. No one will pay on-going what you are not worth. There is nothing more attractive to someone than someone who offers great value and is confident in their self-worth, be it an individual or a company. And there is nothing less attractive than someone needing the sale and discounting their service to get it.

Unique Offerings To Your Market

You need strong collateral (could be your brand, results or other proof) if you want high fees and currency flow. The strength of your collateral is directly linked to the perceived risk to the lender, customer or investor.

A high-value, unique collateral offering decreases risk and increases confidence in you, your products and your services and increases the flow of money to you. The more unique it is, the more it stands out against the also- rans and the higher the perceived value. Collateral has its own section later in the book.

You Are Your Market

Workshop attendees frequently tell me that their market is restricted or has a ceiling. I'm told that they can't charge higher fees in their price- competitive industry; there's just no way, and they would lose business. They could be an accountant, a solicitor, a coach or consultant, or whatever. But if price is what you pay and value is what you get, and we pay more for higher perceived value, then as long as perceived value can be increased, so can fees.

There is a hairdresser in London that charges minimum £5,000 a haircut. There is a restaurant that serves a $1,000 burger. Harry Winston will sell you a pair of shoes for over £50,000. A London solicitor or expert divorce lawyer's fees could run into the millions. Dyson gets us to pay £400+ for a small, digital vacuum cleaner. There are celebrity dogwalkers that charge thousands.

The point is, if you are price focused, you are a commoditised business that will have a price-competitive nature, and your margins will get smaller and smaller as you compete on price. However if you focus on the value proposition, uniqueness of offering and most importantly your own self-worth to execute, you will smash through the apparent glass ceilings of your marketplace. Those glass ceilings are perceived (not real), because in every industry there is an individual or business offering that has higher (perceived) value or service, charging ten or a hundred times more than competitors and gaining a much higher profit margin.

I've proven that for years using strategies like personal brand building, where I helped clients to become the perceived expert or go-to person in their industry or market. Many of them have reported multiplying turnover and profits. It's all in positioning and perception in the eyes of the consumer.

But if you really can argue the limitations of your current industry, maybe you have to change your industry now. It is your choice. Remember the importance of the environment for your success.

Spend More Money

You can't save your way to wealth (alone) because it breaks the rules of flow. Flow of money comes from other people, and other people decide where to spend their money. If they can't see fair exchange in spending their money with you, they will spend it with someone else.

You know the person who ducks out of the rounds at the bar or club. They might think they have made a quick gain and saved the cost of a few drinks, but you know what reputation they build and what they are teaching their "friends" and the world. They build a reputation and become known for it, and they restrict the flow of money from others because they teach others they do not offer fair exchange.

Create more flow, spend more, share more and give more. Have faith that you are teaching the world that you offer fair exchange. Remove over attachment to money and speed up the flow to bring more in.

The Speed Of Money

I find is strange now when people tell me that it's 'hard to make money, although it is exactly what I believed before I changed my Wealth DNA and money beliefs. I believe today that attracting wealth is easier than it ever has been, and the main reason is the speed at which money moves. In the pre-coin days, "money" moved as fast as you could cobble a pair of shoes, take them to a farmer and exchange them for the leg of a cow. In the days of coin and cash, money moved at a faster speed as the common medium of exchange, as fast as a deal could be done between two people. Nowadays money moves at the speed of light, through fibre optics over the Internet. You might have heard of high-frequency trading, where trades on markets are placed at high speeds via computers. At the turn of the 21st century, HFT trades had an execution time of several seconds, whereas by 2010 this had decreased to milli- and even microseconds.

Money can disappear off your bank card at the speed of a swipe, you can bank transfer money and it is in someone else's account in milliseconds. You can start a business with a laptop, Internet connection and payment gateway that you can run from a mobile device. That, my friends, you would have called science fiction or magic just a decade or two ago.

You can set up your business faster than ever, with no plant or machinery cost, no requirement for premises, shop fit-outs, with virtual staff on outsourced websites, remote HR and IT and create value without ever turning over any money. There is lower overhead risk, faster access to cash and payments from your customers and faster access to marketing, brand and leads through free social media platforms. And of course, the idea of a geographically restricted market has disappeared altogether. In my e-commerce and online businesses I have customers from all over the world without having to have offices or customer service operations in those countries. If ever there was an age of the fast start Entrepreneur, it is now.

The Value Exchange Matrix

One of the things I wish I had learned at school or at least before I was in my forties is what I call the 'Value Exchange Matrix'. Money, as outlined in this chapter, is just an agreed way to exchange value. So what you are offering in return for money is an important consideration and directly linked to the amount of money you'll receive. It is 'value collateral'. The five levels of the matrix are directly linked to the levels of leverage or how much or little of your personal time you have to use. Well this sounds more complicated than it actually is, so let me show you the matrix and give a few short explanations to every level. Once you are aware of the 'Matrix of Value Exchange', your single aim in your efforts to create Wealth should be to move more of your efforts higher up the matrix. Every level of the matrix has its own rules and laws and path to mastery, but for the discussion in this book this should suffice.

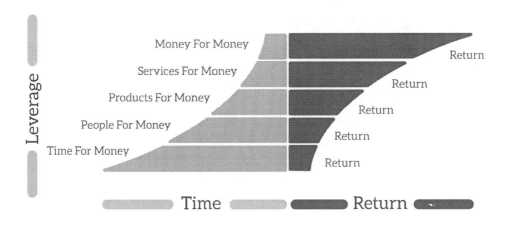

Level 1: Money In Exchange For Time - Leverage You

This is generally the job or self employed level. Yes, you can create more value by upping your skills and becoming a highly paid expert or consultant, and there are a handful of people who get paid a lot of money in high positions, but as a general rule this is classed as the bottom of the matrix because you can't leverage it. If you don't show up, you don't make money. Your time, which is of course limited, is the subject of exchange. I do spend some of my time here - like my £10,000 consulting days or my highly leveraged workshops, but it has limits and is un-leveraged and is at risk from illness, burnout, lack of motivation, industry change or regulation and so on.

Level 2: Money In Exchange For People's Time - Leverage Time

Well, here is where you are a business owner and start to use other people's time to extend your leverage. The secret is simple. You work eight hours a day. If you have two additional employees working eight hours a day for you, you in essence have 24 hours a day, where you create exchangeable value in the marketplace. Systems and processes, key metrics (or KPIs as they are sometimes called) and mastering the skill of managing people and leadership are on the menu. I have a small team of employees, most of them in low- price economies who help me achieve more and control costs. And as I grow and get more human capital, I will earn more on other people's time.

This is how Bill Gates got so rich; he had 50,000 staff all working 10 hours a day for his legacy. That is 50,000 x 8 which is 400,008 hours a day. If on average they bring in £25 an hour each (likely to be more) then that is £10,000,200 a day in income. That is £70,001,400 a week and a year is £3.640073e+9 on my Samsung phone calculator. I guess that's a lot! Bill will show up again in Level 4: Service, as software is one of those cool things you can sell that is highly leverageable.

Level 3: Money In Exchange For Products - Leverage Products

Product-based businesses have the ability to create a high level of wealth but are many times front-loaded and cash-intensive in the start-up phase. Of course, selling products is highly scalable, so making a few bucks from a million units generates a high level of leveraged wealth. You've done the work once and earn on it one million times – better than doing an hour of work then having to do another hour to get the same results, right?

As an additional asset you could be building a high-value brand and loyal customer base that you can get repeat business from and further leverage. My e-commerce business selling private label products using Amazon as a retail channel is a profitable, scalable, product business where I create a brand and loyal customers. I can then sell again and again to those repeat customers, further increasing the leverage. In my case I used an unfair shortcut called white labelling, which means I don't have the lag, cost and risk of developing products.

Level 4: Money In Exchange For Services - Leverage Services

Service-based leverage is similar to products, but is in some ways more attractive as you don't have to ship or sell physical products, and you don't have stock or degradation issues. Service-based exchange can allow you to have recurring subscription income, which is also high predictable. Also scalability is less of an issue than in product based business models with less 'money on the shelves'. My online membership programmes are good examples of the service-based business model. If you can automate the service-based element, for example using online software, video, audio, then you have further leverage. If the service requires manual work that only has a one time benefit, it falls under Level 1. Of course you will be able to see that all very successful individuals or companies use a combination.

Coming back to Bill Gates, it's his Windows operating system at the core that created his wealth, followed by additional services and, only recently, products like the Xbox or Windows phones.

Level 5: Money In Exchange For Money

This is where the big guys make the money: investing money in businesses, projects and ventures. The return can be mind-boggling. I'm not an expert in high finance, but you can create money out of thin air and pay less tax on your profits than at any other level of the matrix! I make some money from this level through private lending, investing for shares or stakes in businesses or joint venture projects. Because money attracts money, you can leverage your money to work hard for you, rather than having to work hard for your money like you do in Level 1. When companies float on the stock market, money is created out of nothing. And if companies buy other companies to increase market share, the multiple of their value increases, again making money out of nothing. Still a mystifying area for me, but I'm determined to get there!

For example, look at banks. They lend out on a factor of 10:1 or up to 20:1 from cash holdings. They get ten or twenty times leveraged investment returns and earn interest not just on the £1 you've given them to look after (and pay you a low return) but on 10x or 20x £1. Check out fractional reserve lending if you want to melt your brain. But that's how the banks got so much money! As money grows, compounding kicks in, the "eighth wonder of the world," according to Albert Einstein, someone smart (and wealthy).

Summary

So there you have it. A short overview of the five levels of the matrix of value exchange. You can use each level as a leg up to the next level, and as you move up each level the good news is you can still get the leveraged benefit of the level you moved up from, further compounding the leverage. The richest people in the world get the benefit of all five, leveraging many people at Level 1, so they can sit at the top of the matrix practicing their Dr. Evil laugh and plotting world domination. Or maybe just finding more ways to help the world! Remember, it's who you already are - magnified.

It's all about knowing how, choosing your vehicles and then leveraging them - and of course keeping an eye on reducing your dependency on trading your time at the bottom of the matrix on Level 1.

Why Dubai Is Actually A Cool Place To Write Wealth DNA

When I decided to write this book in Dubai I did a bit of research on the place. I came out here so that I could get away from the distractions of my world and get this done. And I wanted the right environment; I mean you wouldn't go to Siberia in the middle of winter to write a book on wealth, right?

I guess the most amazing thing about Dubai is just the speed at which it grew to become a major hub for trade. I mistakenly assumed it was the oil that created the wealth; it was in fact creating a favourable tax regime and incentives for global trade that attracted people from all over the world to invest here. And it seems more than fitting to talk about the speed of money in Dubai, so full of wealth yet seemingly so new. Having dinner last night with an estate agent friend of ours, he mentioned the house prices having doubled within a year. The palm (a manmade city in the shape of a palm) was only started in 2001 and partly handed over in 2006. They built a whole futuristic

James Bond-like city in the sea in what seems like the speed of light. Dubai is already called the Hong Kong of the Middle East, and they are currently planning the biggest airport in the world.

One of the secrets of attracting and accumulating wealth is to become a marketplace. It can be either physical like Dubai or virtual like Amazon. And once you control the traffic or footfall, you create an almost monopolistic economy, and you control the money. Well I guess it's true what they say: Build it and they will come.

Why Now Is A Unique Time In History

Is There A Conspiracy To Stop You Being Wealthy?

I don't know where you stand when it comes to conspiracy. Is it really possible that a ruling elite wants to keep the majority of humanity poor and dependent? Is it possible that our schools on purpose neglect their duty to prepare our kids for the real world? Is it possible that schools instead just produce worker bees and pen pushers to run an ever-growing and ever more controlling government? Is it possible that the people controlling mass media misinform us on purpose and fuel superficial desires to buy things we neither want nor need to keep us in debt, so busy making a living that we forget and neglect to build the lives of our dreams?

I sure believed for most of my life that it was almost impossible to live outside the system, and it seems that governments and banks and the powers that be make it impossible to escape. It looks like any western democracy relies on a majority of blue collar and white collar workers to pay high taxes to run the country and pay for the privilege of the welfare state (even though most countries are more limping than running) and have a school system that raises children to fit into their plans, shoe-horn them into the system so they can pay half their earnings in taxes, then cut them out of the system when they become a financial drain later in life. A terrible reality!

As a matter of fact, I don't actually care if there is a conspiracy or not. I could drag out this chapter and look for the proof of these conspiracies, but it is not in the ethos, values and spirit of this book. The reality is that the information age has allowed anyone who wishes to learn all they need to break free from the shackles of the 40/40/40 plan. To work for forty years forty hours a week in a job you don't really like to (hopefully) retire on forty per cent of the money you couldn't even get by on while you were working. All while having more time and needing more money for healthcare and spiralling living expenses!

So - if you live below the line - you can spend your time and effort trying to work out if there is and what kind or conspiracy is controlling the world, or - if you decide to live above the line - you can start changing your Wealth DNA and create resilience from all kinds of possible futures.

The Old System Of Wealth – Taking The Longer View

It might help to take a longer view on society to see how special our times really are. Only a couple of generations ago at the time of your parents and grandparents, society had a pretty rigid structure. There were in essence just three types of people, often also directly linked to the three main classes and distribution of wealth and money in English society.

1. The blue-collar workers, also referred to as working class, who made money with their hands and of course trading their time for money, were at the bottom of society.

2. The white-collar workers or middle classes, who did trade their time for money, but mainly using their mental skills or profession.

3. The upper class, who owned land or other income-producing assets and were the business owners. This is most commonly referred to as old money, as it normally passed down through the generations.

The system was quite rigid and inflexible, and it was almost impossible for a blue or white collar worker to acquire income-generating assets, as these were controlled in an almost impenetrable monopoly held through generations and generations. On top of that, money and the banks were owned and controlled by the same class.

Democratisation Of Wealth - A Revolution

Today everything has changed! The last 30 years have seen a complete democratisation of wealth in all markets - allowing pretty much anybody who wishes to to acquire and accumulate assets and learn about and use the different vehicles of wealth.

There are a few important, overarching developments like the ever- lower cost of technology (due to Moore's law, explained later) and the penetration of the Internet and the linked proliferation of information, that have accelerated this phenomenon.

So let's look at this concept of democratisation of wealth in the different asset classes.

Let Me Start With Property

Many of you will only remember as far back as the last recession and the boom that led up to the recession. I go to property networking meetings and hear people complain about how hard it is to get finance. Really? Compared to what? The fact that we have financial products for buy-to-let mortgages and even multi-let products that pretty much anybody (even with a mediocre credit rating) can get their hands on is a miracle! Buy-to-let mortgages have only been popular since the 1990s as a result of the recession having had many people lose their houses. Today, one in five rental properties is supplied by a private landlord. That is amazing.

I will detail property for you later, as it needs its own section, but the point is that just thirty years ago you had to virtually be a Lord or a Sir to get your hands on property; now TV shows about auctions and doing up rental properties and being a landlord are common daytime viewing and anyone can be a buy-to-let landlord. And while it's now possible, most people make a right mess of it. It's worth learning how to do it right, and I have friends running "Progressive Property," one of the most successful property education companies in the UK.

Let's Look At Trading The Markets

Not too long ago (information about this varies based on my research) it would have cost you tens of thousands to get a trading license and get the financial data to be able to be a broker. I know from friends who have been in the industry for a while, who still remember having paid large five-figure sums a month just to have access to financial data. Today you can get all this for free. And instead of having to invest in expensive software, you can download your trading app from the App Store or Google Play. That is revolutionary. It's science fiction. As they say, any technology advanced enough cannot be distinguished from magic. If you ask me, it's magic. It's definitely beyond the realms of my understanding that I can trade real time from my iPhone while I'm anywhere in the world, walking the dog or sitting on the beach, and make money in my palm or on the Palm (in Dubai, if you get my drift!).

Let's Look At E-Commerce

Like the ability to be trading the markets from your phone, making money online from selling goods and services is so new that your teacher and your parents couldn't have told you about it. It's not just that they didn't know about it. It actually didn't exist! Amazon. com will have hit $100 billion in trade in 2014, looking to double in the next three years, and Amazon is only doing about 15 per cent of e- commerce in the US. EBay and other retail sites can be set up quickly, and you are in business in minutes as long as you have access to the internet - which today means pretty much all the time using a smartphone.

Amazon's projected growth will come from the democratisation of its seller platform, taking away most of the pain of making money online when selling physical products. Again, if I had told my Dad just a few years ago what you and I can do today, he would have thought I'd smoked the 'crazy tobac' as he called it!

Running Your Own Business

The UK has come out of recession. It will go in again and come out again and go in again. According to reports, though, the last time was the first time that people actually didn't want to go back to work and get a job. Instead, many went out to start their own businesses. The reasons are many-fold, from the mobile world of the Internet to the lower cost of starting a business. They'd gotten fed up of being exploited and being taken advantage of. Fair play to those that went out and did something about it. I was one of them!

Here are the stats: In 2006 there were 145,104 companies started – by 2014 this number had jumped to 247,049 – almost double!

And although there are many horror stories and numbers being passed around of how many businesses fail within the first year, first five years and so on, on average 50 per cent of businesses are still trading after five years. Businesses in the finance, property and insurance sectors top the charts with 58 per cent, and businesses in the information sector are at the bottom with 37 per cent. My guess is that people entering the information sector are attracted by the low startup threshold and are less prepared and more naïve, but for sure it is a growing market. Also don't underestimate people winding down their businesses for many reasons, including the very attractive entrepreneurs' relief, which allows any entrepreneur to take up to £10 million of earnings at a mere 10 per cent tax bracket. Check the small print, and talk to your adviser team.

Another really interesting set of numbers is around the amount of money needed to start a business. Although the average cost of starting a traditional business is around £94,000, the number for a micro-business is just £41,000, and 76 per cent of online businesses have been started with less than £2,000 of start-up funds!

So running your own business is pretty much a must if you want to be wealthy. I'm not even gonna go into all the advantages from a tax perspective at this point or the VAT (you can even register before you reach the threshold) that you could claim back on most things you buy – just re-read Rich Dad, Poor Dad to remind yourself of the main difference of paying expenses before you pay tax compared to living from taxed-earned income.

Overarching Trends

I mentioned in my introduction to this chapter that there are some overarching developments, like the high level of penetration of the Internet and decreasing cost of technology. There is a third factor, which makes all of this even more attractive and compelling: global trade! Being able to buy in China or the Philippines and sell in the Americas or Western Europe is a new opportunity. If you had attempted to import from China ten or twenty years ago, it would have been a major headache requiring deep pockets and a unique set of skills and contacts. Today it's open season for all. Instead of ordering container loads full of stuff, you can get smaller and smaller quantities, reducing cost and risk. There is a reason why alibaba.com, the Chinese e-commerce website, was the hottest IPO in 2014!

Digital printing makes customisation and branding affordable and being able to outsource to countries where the average wage is a fraction of the cost in Europe creates that perfect storm.

No more stories, no more excuses. No more blame, complain, justify. It's the best time ever in the history of mankind to make some moolah! The world has opened its doors to do business. Walk right through, my friend!

What Is The Wealth Diamond?

Now that you understand what a special time in history this is and why you really have to be wealthy to live a life of meaning and fulfilment, let's talk about my Wealth Diamond. I created the Wealth Diamond to put the complex concepts of how to create lasting wealth into a simple model. I think you'll love the simplicity of it, and at the same time you'll appreciate the depth and completeness of the model. Its aim is to give you an overview and system to follow of everything you need to equip you on your journey to change your Wealth DNA - to create the life you deserve and desire using the proven principles of lasting wealth.

The way we learn as human beings is not just about information, but also about the context of information. That is why it's very useful to create a model of learning or remembering systems, process, strategies and general information. Using metaphors, analogies or stories really helps us humans to create meaning and deeper understanding and increase future retention and recall. Ever since Roger Sperry's work on the brain hemispheres in the late '60s, we have known that our left and right brain fulfil quite different functions. While the left brain is processing logical and sequential information, the right brain is better at processing abstract and visual information. So when I set out to put the knowledge of Wealth DNA into a model, I ended up with the Wealth Diamond...

The Wealth Diamond
Wealth DNA

So Why A Diamond?

Well I'm glad you asked. There are many great lessons that I can weave in from the diamond. Firstly it's a great symmetric geometric shape. So it's easy to draw and remember. But there is more. The word diamond from its Greek root means "unbreakable" or "lasting," so when I set out to write a book on the proven principles of lasting wealth, the diamond model was the perfect shape. And lasting means unbreakable, hence the subtitle of the book.

Another fascinating fact about the diamond is that it the hardest mineral known to man, ranking as a 10 on the Mohs scale. A diamond is also one of the most valuable minerals in the world, and as the say in the James Bond film, "Diamonds Are Forever."

It's also noteworthy that graphite, which is one of the softest materials with a 1-2 on the Mohs scale of mineral hardness, is made out of the same core material as a diamond: carbon. The symbol for carbon is C, so when I share with you the 4 Cs of the Wealth Diamond, you'll see how it is all connected. And to add to the fascination and comparison with you changing your Wealth DNA, a diamond is charcoal, or carbon, that handled intense pressure really well. And the analogy carries on: only the right kind of pressure in the right environment will create a diamond. I think it's genius!

What I found out when I started researching diamonds is that there is a phenomenon called price jumping that pretty much states that the price of a diamond, based on its carat (another C) or weight (or value, if you want to create the analogy to business), does not go up in a linear fashion. It actually jumps from level to level, with an ever-increasing value per weight class.

Diamond Prices From 0.08ct to 1.00ct
Wealth DNA

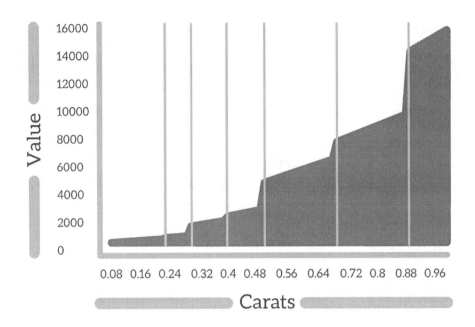

This is just like what I observed in business, when you move from £100k to £250k, from £250k to £500k, from £500k to £1m and so on... In business this is normally put down to momentum, but the reality is that value of your business does not grow in a linear way. It grows in a compounded way, and the longer you've been going and the more momentum you have, the easier it is to achieve 10 or 100 times more.

This is just like a rocket, which uses fully 80 per cent of its entire fuel just to get off the ground. Then it simply flies in space on its momentum.

So when I introduce the contents of the Wealth Diamond to you, you'll see that it consists of the 4 Cs, which stand for Cashflow, collateral, character and communication. When you understand and start using the 4 Cs, your Wealth DNA will change. Even knowing about the 4Cs will start the change!

Just like the 4Cs of the Wealth Diamond will determine your Wealth DNA, so does the value of a diamond.

The 4 C's Of A Diamond That Determine Its Value

The 4 Cs of a diamond are carat, cut, colour and clarity. If you look at what creates value in a diamond and what creates value in a human being who created wealth, you can see strong similarities.

Carat

Carat (or the weight of a diamond) is the most important component of its valuation and can be compared to net worth. Wealthy people do not compare turnover, profit or salaries; they compare their net worth. And just like a diamond's value jumps in levels, so does the net worth of the wealthy, because at the highest level of the matrix of value exchange, money makes more money through compounding and leverage.

Colour

The second ingredient that determines the value of a diamond is colour. Interestingly, the colour in a diamond stems from other ingredients or minerals, and some colours are more rare than others. Of course the simple law of scarcity determines that more rare colours are more valuable. If I wanted to compare the colour of a diamond to a real world business example, I would say that the colour is like how you appear to the world. The brand you create, the online avatar you choose to represent yourself or your company in the world and the reputation you create are much like the colour of a diamond. But unlike the diamond, you can choose and adjust how you appear in the world.

Cut

The third component is the cut. This is the one component that is most influenced by the human interaction with the gem. Its weight, colour and clarity are a given (just like the seed, sand and soil from our earlier example), but what you do with it is the magic that adds the value. An experienced diamond cutter will have a choice of many shapes, aiming to maximise the value, and the quality and experience of his cutting will make the difference. So how does that relate to you and your Wealth DNA? I compare the cut of a diamond to the cloth you cut from. The mindset, the attitude, the character you create and shape to face the challenges and exploit the opportunities the world offers you.

If you say you are "cut from the same cloth" as someone, you refer to sharing ideas, opinions, beliefs and passions. We'll spend more on mindset and beliefs later in the book, but that is one of the most important parts of changing your Wealth DNA - changing the ideas, values and beliefs. In its historical context, the clothes you wore were made from very different types of cloth depending on your status and wealth. And even today you can see what clothes you are wearing (the brands you choose to represent yourself in the world) or cars you are driving or area you are living in are closely linked to the status and level of wealth the represent.

Clarity

The last component and 4th C that determines the value of a diamond is clarity. The flawless perfection of a crystal clear stone is the pursuit. And if you want to relate that very same concept to the world of Wealth and the Wealth Diamond, it would be the clarity of your legacy living through purpose, creating vision through others and the communication, which determines much of the value of your enterprise.

The vision of an entrepreneur, where he or she wants to take the company and the mission he or she wants to accomplish by getting there, has become more important in the last few decades. We are as interested in the person behind the mission and the vision as we are the mission and vision. The Internet revolution has also presented us with a new transparency that cuts both ways. It exposes you if you do bad, but it also exposes if you do good. So the clarity of your vision and mission, the way you lead your life and your enterprise, your legacy through purpose and the way you communicate that vision using your marketing channels creates value by itself and enhances the value of your enterprise.

In the next section we'll delve into the Wealth Diamond and its 4 Cs. That's when you'll discover the vehicles and the other components of lasting, unbreakable wealth. And just like charcoal in the right environment under the right pressure becomes a diamond, so will you transform yourself into the most valuable version of yourself, and the most powerful Wealth DNA.

The Wealth Diamond: The 1st C – Cashflow

The first of the 4 Cs is cashflow. Of course it would come first, because life force in finance is liquidity. And if cash is king, as they say, then cashflow is God. Cash, of course, flows both ways, and you can increase what you keep by controlling what you spend and reduce unnecessary outgoings. In this chapter we'll concern ourselves a lot more with cash flowing to you, not the flow of cash away from you, called cost, overheads or expenses. Cashflow as part of the Wealth Diamond concerns itself with the incoming flow. Cashflow can be active income (like a job), or passive income

89

from assets, which in my view is the real definition. After all, it has the word "flow" attached to the end of it, not cash-labour or cash-graft or cash-slave. So to restate, cashflow is income from assets.

Most people in the world are employed and have a job. And pretty much all of them would like more freedom and choice in life and like the idea of quitting their job to get more passive income. You might be one them. If you are one of the rare individuals who loves their job and lives their legacy living through purpose at their job, then that's great. But it is rare. Most people are working too hard to get rich, exchanging the little time they have for just enough money to survive, delaying all holidays, privileges and happiness, in the hope that one day when they are old they can retire, and then they die shortly after. And their job does not allow them to fulfil their vision, live their purpose or create a lasting legacy. If that sounds familiar, then read on.

Job or employed income is just one level up from no income, also known as slavery. The employee has an illusion of security in a regular wage to pay the bills, yet their employer could fire them at any time, their role could become redundant, their services a relic, their pay rises are not matching inflation and they have no control of when or where they work. Remember the day you wanted to take a holiday or a break and the boss said no? Well, sorry for reminding you. It's humiliating and frustrating and just shows you your place.

In my experience from training and speaking to tens of thousands of people, it is the lack of freedom of choice as much as if not more than the lack of money that hurts most people, the feeling of being trapped in the rat race as a wage slave and working thirty days in arrears because expensive bills, school fees and direct debits have to be paid on the first of each month, with virtually all the month left at the end of the money. That is how close most of them are, often just a few days, to running out of money and savings and being personally 'insolvent'. It is living each month with living expenses at more than 100 per cent of income, so debts compound each day, getting bigger and bigger to the point where it hangs like a black cloud wherever you go, raining on every part of your life, hoping for another 0 per cent credit card offer to come through the letterbox. I know - I've been there. It sucks.

Having a lack of cash makes it hard to give your kids what you want to give them; it makes it hard to have an amazing relationship, and having no money consumes your thoughts negatively and makes it hard to be present and grateful. It's true that rich people and wealthy people have their attention on money and talk about money, but from having been there, so do the poor and broke - but in a negative and destructive way.

There are two types of cash: capital and income. In each of the two types there are different levels. Your goal would be to rise up through the levels of capital and income to go from (earned) active, occurring income through to passive, recurring income. From exchanging time for money to making your money work hard for you.

Cash Type 1: Capital
Capital is a cash lump. It's stash of cash in your safe. It's the notes stuffed under your mattress. It has no income element (at the moment), it is a hoard of money. It provides a level of security and liquidity.

Cash Type 2: Income
Income is cash-flow. Income is liquid cash moving inwards and

outwards. It is recurring cash. It is not as lumpy as capital, but regular, sustainable and predictable. It is currency movement. It is defined in the Oxford Dictionary as "money received, especially on a regular basis, for work or through investments." An added layer of security above capital is income, and when you have enough passive income from your capital base, you have time and financial freedom.

Levels Of Cash Type 1 - Capital

Level 1. Cash

The basic level of capital is cash. Cash can be in physical form, such as money or gold, or intangible such as in a bank account, bonds or low- yield, low-risk assets such as ISAs or "tracker" stocks and shares. It has to be liquid, otherwise it doesn't act as protection (because you can't access it fast enough), but the trade-off is that it generates a relatively low return (or negative returns if it is not inflation shielded or is in volatile markets).

As tempting as it is to move all cash-based capital into higher yielding investments, you reduce liquidity and therefore increase risk of irregular shocks or large cash hits/drains hurting you. Having large piles of cash has its benefits and drawbacks; ideally you have around a year's living expenses in liquid cash assets. Any more and the low return burns the capital; any less and you might not be liquid enough for irregular shock protection. If you currently have zero or one month's protection through cash, make it part of your plan – you'll feel better for it. Just assign a small portion of your income to this pot.

Level 2. Assets

Assets are owned 'property', that have retained value in excess of the debt value. An asset produces income; it is the tree from which the fruits of income fall and flow and grow. It is the security for a loan, the protection mechanism for the income to flow from. Many people refer to many of their possessions as assets, even they are actually liabilities! Here is the simple test of whether or not something's an asset: Does it put money in your pocket? If not, it's a liability.

Level 3. Equity

Equity is the net value of the asset minus the debt attached to it. It is, for example, your property value after cost of loan and capital. It is the retained net value, what would be paid back to you as profit after a sale or disposal, after the deduction of charges. An over- geared asset isn't actually an asset.

For an asset to be an asset it must have equity and income. Equity forms a large amount of your net worth. A property millionaire has a £1 million-plus property portfolio value, but if that has 90 per cent debt then the equity portion is only £100,000. That would be the net worth or value of the portfolio. The same portfolio owned outright with no debt would have £1 million equity value.

Levels Of Cash Type 2 - Income

Level 1. Earned income (Employee/Job)

Money received in exchange for time, work or sweat. Refer to the start of this section.

What's Wrong With A Job?

I'm not asking you to quit your job tomorrow, and it makes sense to be employed in your own company for tax purposes – but you have to be realistic about the likelihood of that job income giving you financial freedom, stability and security. The likelihood is close to zero to be blunt with you.

But what sucks most about most jobs is not just that people are selling their time for money. It's about doing something that doesn't inspire them with people they might not want to be with in an environment they didn't choose. That is the soul crushing aspect of many jobs. You do them just to make enough money to get by and you are just a couple of pay cheques away from being broke. I know - I've been there, for two decades of my life. And that creates fear and uncertainty I will remember forever.

Long hours are not a problem if you are in flow. No one has to clock you in and clock you out from what you love to do. Have you ever been with a person you love doing what you love and thought to yourself, "Shit. That's a long day"? Of course not! So it's not the quantity of time you are spending – it's the quality.

My good friend Rob Moore is up at 5 A.M. every day working until late. These are long days. But it's not just passion that drives him; he's driven by a legacy, purpose and vision. That is very different to working night shifts at Domino's Pizza.

Level 2. Turnover (Business)
The gross amount of money taken by a business, normally measured yearly; sometimes monthly. It is all income from all sources before cost of sales, fixed costs (overheads) and variable costs are taken off. Turnover is total cash generated in one-off lumps, commissions or in recurring billings or payment plans. Turnover is cash and lifeblood of any business, but it is also the vanity of a business, the number shared in conversations and from stage or when you are comparing your company with your peers. It's not that indicative for the health of your business. You could be turning over millions and be insolvent, living the life of a zombie business, meaning your are a 'living dead' business, surviving month on month without profit,

just paying salaries and interests on debt.

Level 3. Profit (Turnover Minus All Expenses)

Profit is turnover minus costs. Gross profit is turnover minus cost of sales (the costs to bring in the sales such as commissions). Net profit is gross profit minus all costs (fixed and variable). There is an old saying, "If turnover is vanity then net profit is sanity." Net profit is what you make before taxes and is more of a measure of the reality of your income position than turnover; though high turnover has additional benefits even with low(er) profit margins, such as increase in capital value or market share perception.

Level 4. Net Cashflow (Income Minus Expenses)

Net cashflow is income minus expenses. In your property business it is rental income minus cost of finance, management and other income-related costs such as maintenance and voids. It is cash in your bank minus corporation tax and personal tax and national insurance. It is dividends from stocks and shares minus commissions and taxes. So as a more modern saying goes, "If turnover is vanity and profit is sanity then net cashflow is the reality." It's what you get to finance your lifestyle.

Level 5. Tax Reduction

Tax reduction is a form of income, in that there is more left over from turnover, profit and net cashflow. The more you make, the more it'll pay to understand how different company structures can save you tax (and increase profit), what you can legitimately offset, save or roll up and ways you can re-invest cash to shield it from the taxation (which is drawing it out).

No point paying an expensive London-based tax specialist when you earn £15,000 a year, but as your business grows it will pay big to get smart tax advice and organise your corporate structures and strategies around the most efficient tax position. If you bring £1 into your business through turnover, it will likely cost you 50p-plus in taxes (corporation and then income) and national insurance (employers and employees), whereas if you save £1 then you "make" the entire £1.

I remember meeting with an offshore specialist in London's Landmark Hotel in 2009 for a chat about saving taxes. His advice was clear: "Make (a lot) more money, then come back to me!" Good advice. I remember it vividly, and my business partner James and I have recalled the meeting many times since. Too many people worry about paying taxes on money they haven't earned yet. Make some money, pay your taxes, then make more money and start paying fewer taxes (in relative terms). The reality and good news is the wealthiest people pay the least taxes in per cent of income.

As you progress up Levels 1-3 in the equity cash type and Levels 1-5 in the income cash type, not only do you become seriously wealthy, you also have eight levels and layers of protection for lasting, unbreakable wealth. Your Wealth DNA will have a new coding, and your life and legacy will have changed forever.

Cashflow Models

You already know that I believe it is easier than ever before to create wealth and do it fast! There are many different models for creating equity and income. You can become a master of one, or you can use multiple income models for compounded income and equity. You might choose a model that fits your legacy living through purpose, or you might choose a model because it seems the most conducive to your desired life, then use the equity and income to live your legacy or because it provides the fastest route to where you need to be.

Model 1. Earned Income (Employee/Job)

Money received in exchange for time, work or sweat. Refer to the start of this section.

Model 2. Royalty Income

Royalty income is recurring, passive income from a physical (tangible) or non-physical (intangible) asset. It is a passive share of the overall profits on a recurring basis, each time the asset is used, rented or bought. Royalty income is income that keeps coming in from an asset that was created once, so it has a residual element. If you are fortunate or skilled enough to have written a Christmas No. 1, you will get paid big each Christmas when the song rules the airwaves. The artist receives a share of the profits from sales and a share of the license fee the radio and TV stations pay to use the song. It can last decades, too. The creator could be a songwriter who isn't part of the band or a playwright or composer.

Royalty income is work once and get paid forever (or over and over). Owning intellectual property is pretty much like owning physical property. Many of you might not know this, but for a lot of my life I was really into music, and writing songs and it was actually my plan for becoming wealthy doing something I loved. The plan was to get a record deal and get paid royalties forever. No further work required.

As a matter of fact I had one of my songs in the Austrian charts in 1994 and I'm still getting a humble royalty cheque every year. It's not much – but it's free money and another leveraged income stream. It really is amazing. I don't know who listens to my music, but somehow they play it a few times every year, and I get paid. Imagine having a worldwide No. 1 or indeed – a Christmas No. 1! You would get hundreds of thousands of pounds, maybe millions.

A crazy story: have you ever seen the film The Third Man? It's an Orson Welles movie set in Vienna, but it's partly famous for a song written and played on a zither (an Austrian string instrument) by Anton Karas. I saw an interview with the guy who wrote that song back in the 1949, who still received yearly royalties in excess of £50,000 a year, sixty-five years later, for one memorable riff in one film! If I can crack the code of this and work out the system, I will let you know in my next book, Songwriting DNA – How to Write a Christmas No. 1 and Get Paid Forever.

So royalty income is a great income, but to publish music and get money from airplay is not very easy to influence and control, or maybe just not your vocation or passion.

But a similar income stream is royalty income from books. Well, the fact I'm writing my fourth right now (you're reading it!) might give you a clue that it's a worthwhile pursuit and that it's not that hard. You can choose to sell them via Amazon or sell them yourself from events or your website and office. And these days you don't even need a publisher!

My book sales income (not including this one) is nothing to retire on, but this month it was over £500 from book sales. Who wouldn't take £6,000 every year for work you've done once, many years ago? And the fact that the book is a strategic product for my business adds to the fun, of course!

Even if you don't sell hundreds of books and it never become an Amazon bestseller, it might be worth writing a book just on the impact on your authority positioning and expert status in your industry.

I think it makes sense to have many different independent and interdependent income streams. Everyone I know who is wealthy has multiple income streams. None of them just have a job income. And although it's a good idea to be known for one thing in the marketplace from a marketing perspective, you should make money from many different sources. In my case, I make money from property. I've got royalty income. I make money from e-commerce. I run multiple kinds of conventional trading businesses, like my training and coaching business, and I also invest in joint ventures, leveraging the skills and experience of other smart people and making money from my money. You can use virtually all the income streams listed and about to be listed in multiple niches or marketplaces and add them all together.

Look at Jamie Oliver. He's obviously good at cooking. But his main income comes from other sources: he does TV shows on cooking. He writes books and has recorded audio books on cooking. Now he's got apps for smartphones (one of his most lucrative income streams, I heard). He licenses his name to supermarkets and restaurants and collects TV advertising revenue, all from cooking. According to the Sunday Times Rich List, his net worth is around $400 million.

But don't feel you have to miss out on this income stream if you are not a learned (notice, not born) artist or musician or chef. Royalty income can come - as discussed - in the form of a book or audio programme (via a publisher). But you can also create media like an e-book on Kindle or audio book version. Then you will have three IP assets that create a royalty income. Each time Amazon, Audible or iTunes sell one of your audios, you get a share of the profits. You could create a training manual or DVD set from the same knowledge, which also falls into e-commerce and IP, but if you are using a shop or promoter to sell the products for you, you get a recurring royalty payment. And the apps market for smartphones is estimated to be worth $35 billion in 2014 alone. Opportunity? You bet.

You could create a patent on an idea you have (IP), and each time the user uses the patented product or idea, you get a royalty income. Ruben Rausing created Tetra Pak in 1951, a company that founded a series of innovations around packaging that created a revenue in 2012 alone of 11.155 billion Euros and an empire of 23,425 staff.

Here is another example of how the license or royalty from IP can be worth billions. The Post-It note was accidentally created from a failed glue in 1977, and the patent that lasted 20 years made 3M hundreds of billions. Despite the original patent running out in 1997, the famous yellow colour and name is still owned by 3M, and 2013 revenues for 3M were $30.87 billion.

Model 3. Intellectual Property (IP)

Intellectual property (IP) is the ownership of an intangible asset such as a patent or copyright. It is the asset that produces the royalty income. A patent can be an idea, a product, a particular way of doing something, a process (that can be franchised), an innovation, a logo, a film or an image (photograph, image rights of a person).

One of the most powerful, fastest and most accessible forms of IP is information. My specialised field in business is information marketing, where concepts, ideas and information have an asset value and can be sold or rented, in the forms already stated such as a book, audiobook, Kindle, CD, DVD, training manual, training course, mentorship programme, legacy programme, membership site and more. You can even introduce some of that value onto your balance sheet and draw income tax efficiently if you are running a company structure like an LLP in the UK. Talk to a specialist accountant about what that could mean for your net worth and tax position.

It took you many years of your life and a huge investment of money and time to become a specialist or expert in your field. Now you can call in income on it, in virtually all forms (capital, income, royalty) for the rest of your life. You or your knowledge becomes the (insurable) asset that backs the recurring income. I call this model the "product staircase" in information marketing, where you escalate the value of the information and the medium in which you deliver it, for a higher income at each step. Even if you are not the most experienced or most knowledgeable person in your industry or in the world, using some of the marketing knowledge I share in my courses goes a long way towards letting the world know that you are an expert and getting paid handsomely for it.

Let me give you a real world practical example of some product staircases from my businesses. The idea of a product staircase is that people can transact with you at low risk and low expense, and you then take the most interested and most qualified people to the next level, increasing the value you give them, and at the some time changing the delivery mechanism of the information and increasing your fees.

At the beginning of running my training and information marketing business back in 2006 I only had a single one-day workshop and I sold it from live events that marketing partners put on. I paid the marketing partners 50 per cent of sales. That is not a product staircase!

So after a couple of years of just selling workshops (a leveraged model, but not passive of course) I created a next level workshop at a higher price and shortly later a yearlong continuation coaching programme I called the 'academy'. The academy was split into different levels (Gold, Platinum, Diamond) to allow pretty much anyone to find their own right level of commitment and investment and level of peer group. This model is a valuable and profitable way to diversify your product offering, as I also encouraged members to move up the staircase to the higher level as they and their income grew. This also allowed me to use the advanced selling strategy of contrast selling and the alternative close ("Both levels will get you great results, you can choose either Platinum or Diamond..."), which increased my turnover and profit dramatically, while at the same time helping my clients achieve more. At the top of the group staircase I created an Inner Circle Mastermind Group, which was limited to just 12 businesses and therefore the most expensive level.

One of the wonderful side effects of having a staircase like that is that some people will want more time with you, which will lead to one-to-one consultancy, which I currently charge out at £10,000 a day, which for the right business is very good value.

I got most of my customers from speaking on someone else's stage (which is a low-risk way to acquire customers) and referrals from existing customers, so a complete product staircase also needs a prospect conversion piece: a low-level, low-risk introductory offer. Books are great products for that purpose, so I wrote Expert Success Formula and Expert Success Stories. If writing books sounds too daunting or onerous to you, you can also start to run one-day or half- day discovery or training events. Voila – a complete staircase.

Importantly, you don't have to create all steps all at once, and against much of the commonly given advice from people in the industry who suggest you build them from the ground up, I normally advise people to start in the middle then go up and finally create the front end. The reason is that in most cases it takes quite a lot of time to create the front end and the low price point, which means you have to do a high volume of sales (which has its own challenges, of course) to generate some decent income. So it's actually easier to start with your £500 to £2,000 workshop (depending on length, content and the market you're operating in) and take it from there. Think about it: Just selling ten places on a workshop for £1,000 is £10,000 for a weekend's work. I regularly run workshops with 50 people for £2,000 a person, creating a whopping £100,000 for a weekend.

So after a few years I had the complete staircase: online offers to buy the low-price book with bonus stack, preview/discovery day, workshop, multi-level academy, private one-to-one clients; from free, to £10, to £500, to £2,000 to £12,000 a year to a £10,000 one-to- one consulting day.

This might look or sound overwhelming to start with, and you might wonder how big a team you'll need to run this and how much you'll be able to make from a business like that. I ran this business with one business partner, one PA and a part-time coach, and we turned over around £600,000 with very low cost and therefore high profit in year two from startup.

I'm also a business partner in the self-development company Unlimited Success (US for short). In Unlimited Success we have a similar staircase, but it's worth sharing it with you so you can see the differences and almost unlimited (see what I did there?) opportunities.

Unlimited Success is an events business. Simply put, the events are split into a series of free discovery events and then paid delivery events. All the marketing efforts are to encourage people to attend a three-day live event called Wealth Breakthrough Live or one of the one-day discovery days on specialized subject matters. We give lots of great free and low-cost information and inspiration (much like the contents of this book – if you like this, you'll be blown away by our live trainings) and often offer low-cost or free tickets to Wealth Breakthrough Live if small investments are made in books or audio programmes. So we prove ourselves to you first in free or low-cost transactions.

The staircase looks like this: Three times a year we are creating a new low-price product or service like a book (for example, the one you are reading now), a CD set or similar high perceived value but low production cost physical product. The aim is to get great information that can change people's lives and they can instantly use, for low cost and risk to them and low cost and risk to us.

They are physical products so they have real value to the customer (unlike e-books that just clog up hard drive space), and we acquire the complete postal address details of our customers, which allows us to do more impactful marketing and share more messages of value in more than one (email) medium.

These low price, high value products are sold at a great discount to encourage the purchase at the speed of light. Our philosophy is that we are not looking to make money from this first step. We don't want to lose money (a strategy called a loss-leader I don't subscribe to and wouldn't recommend unless you know the value of your back end transaction and value per customer), but we are investing in acquiring a new customer and, more importantly, the trust from the new customer who has thousands of messages pummelled over their heads every day.

Part of these prices and high-value purchases (sometimes a P&P offer, which simply means the client just pays for postage, packaging and a small admin fee) is always a bonus VIP ticket to one of our Wealth Breakthrough Live events. Tickets to these events are worth hundreds of pounds in real value, so people appreciate receiving them as part of their low-price purchase. As good as books are, and they have their place, you don't get the real, human experience, the connection and trust, the humour, the ability to ask and answer personal questions. This is why I love live events, because there is literally no other medium where true transformation occurs so rapidly, with such certainty in such an inspiring and supportive environment. I love running them and I love attending them to further my learning.

So the events are where all the magic happens. It is where we connect, where we meet and get to know each other, looking into each other's eyes to see if there is a fit or partnership worth investing in. Unlike many multi-speaker events in our industry, we don't have lots of speakers selling conflicting products where you are asked to run to the back of the room every 90 minutes, 45 minutes of which was a big sales pitch. There are just three speakers at Wealth Breakthrough Live: myself, Rob Moore (multi-millionaire empire builder) and Dillon Dhanecha (a very successful Forex trader and global social entrepreneur). We are all great friends, business partners, doing what we love and helping you achieve the same.

We have created a unique, inspirational and educational 3-day experience with experts who are not just making their money by teaching (you'd be surprised and shocked how many do), but actually running their own business doing what they teach. The events are in essence low cost to free to the attendee, and we only offer a handful of courses for sale should people choose to want to learn more, without the pressure and hype. The ones who understand the value of on-going investment in themselves and really want to create Wealth and legacy join 'Expert Speaker Revolution', the 'Progressive Property Investing Masterclass', the 'Amazon Millionaire Masterclass' or the 'One Hour Trading Academy'. We combine the mindset and skillset so you're not left upset. The cheese is thrown in at no extra cost ;-)

This multi-step selling has proven to be quite effective. On average we are turning over between £1,200 and £2,400 per attendee, so on an event with 100 delegates you can work out the numbers. There is obviously a lot of effort that goes into filling events like this, but it's a highly profitable model you can adopt.

I love the money, but the best thing for me is all is the love, gratitude and success stories created from Wealth Breakthrough Live; it is truly humbling to have a successful business model and make a real difference, too.

I can't even begin to describe how different that makes me feel compared to doing IT training for Hewlett Packard. I can't recall a single one of my HP customers thanking me for having changed their life after I trained them on our software!

Model 4. Property

roperty is the tangible, physical bricks and mortar asset of rental properties in residential or commercial form. The residential (personal living) or commercial (business) property is an asset that (if managed and geared correctly) produces recurring income. Property is one of the safest assets because it has long-term utility.

It can be used for hundreds of years, therefore increasing in value at least with inflation, because it will still have utility hundreds of years from now.

A computer will not have the same utility because of Moore's law (the doubling of the number of transistors in a circuit every two years, thus doubling the power/processing speed, thus devaluing the predecessor dramatically or even rendering it useless and worthless). Virtually everything you buy has its own Moore's law, where its utility diminishes in a relatively short period of time compared to physical property. It is this long-term utility that makes property a safe proposition for the banks to use it as security for loans.

They don't say "safe as the stock market," they say "safe as houses." The banks won't lend to you and use your bicycle your stock portfolio as security/guarantee, but they will lend using a property as security.

Because of its long utility, property goes up in value steadily and consistently over time. Prices would have to stay relative to wages (it would be weird if milk and a house cost the same), and wages are (relatively) pushed up by inflation. This virtually guarantees a steady rise in property prices, before factoring in forced growth through regeneration, ripple effects and supply versus demand implications and, of course, all the creative buying and value-add strategies you can learn and use.

Since 1952, when average UK property prices were £1,891, property has steadily risen, though not always in a linear fashion, where in 2014 the average property price (according to the office of national statistics) was £274,000. In fact one of my business partners Mark Homer, who manages most of my property affairs, managed to track prices back to 1088 (that's the kind of guy he is), where UK land and property valuation was levied for taxation purposes. The total land and property value in the UK almost a millennium ago was just under £1 million. Today a one-bed flat in Chelsea in London costs more than that! That is average yearly growth of 10 per cent.

Ten per cent growth is a reasonable to good return. It is a good return relative to the low-risk nature of most property investments. But it's not the full, or best part of the story. The 10 per cent return is without leverage (debt creating equity). If a property has a £10,000, 10 per cent deposit and a value of £100,000 (figures for ease not indicative), the 10 per cent return on the property after a year would be £10,000, giving it a total value of £110,000. But that is a 10 per cent return on the property, not a 10 per cent return on investment (ROI). The (simplified) ROI would be 100 per cent (gross); because only 10 per cent was put down as a deposit to secure the asset, the remaining 90 per cent loaned by the bank or private/JV partner, yet the return (growth) was on the full value of the asset. And that is all yours to keep.

Of course you have to take off cost of finance (debt) and other costs to get the net return, but this return is exceptional and realistic. If you then raised the 10 per cent deposit from a different financier (private investor, loan), then you have infinite ROI, because it took none of your capital to get a £10,000 return on value (10 per cent of £100,000). This compounds upwards because the next year (year two), 10 per cent of £110,000 is £11,000. Better still, the debt on the property through mortgage stays at a fixed amount and is therefore eroded by inflation over time. In year two the debt is still only £90,000, which relatively is worth around 5 per cent less due to inflation erosion. So in year two not only do you have year one return and year two return (10 per cent higher than year 1), you also have 5 per cent less relative debt, giving you more NET equity. Amazing?

Brain hurting? Mind boggled? Let's use a different part of our brain for a moment. Look at your left hand and admire the little hairs on the back of it. Wow! Fascinating. Nature is so cool! Amazing. Now take a deep breath. Grrreat. Ready to carry on? Yes sir!

So – where were we? In addition to the asset-based return, you have an income stream attached to property, too, in the form of rental income. Both residential and commercial property produce rental income, in the form of gross rent roll and net rental income after debt, management and other income-related costs, such as maintenance, voids and service charges.

Yields (or gross income as a per centage of the value) on good property investments can range from 6 per cent to 15 per cent. It can be less in a more expensive area, and more in a lower value area or with an innovative model such as Multi-Let or Rent2Rent. Once you take off all costs including payment of interest, you could be left with a 1-5 per cent net yield or more. So on the same £100,000 property where you are getting an infinite ROI, 10 per cent return on value (ROV), you could also be getting 3 per cent net regular income stream (£3,000 a year). When you multiply that by ten properties, you have a job replacing passive income minus all costs but before taxes, and you have a seven-figure gross asset base and six-figure net asset base or net worth. Many of my friend Rob's students have done this in 12 months or less.

There are many streams of income and models you can implement for Capital, Equity and Income through property. This is not a property book, so I recommend 'Multiple Streams of Property Income', best selling property book by Rob Moore, for all the models around property. The main strategies and income property models that I personally use to build my Wealth are Buy to Sell (B2S), Buy to Let (B2L - residential and commercial), HMO (House of Multiple Occupancy or Multi-Let) and Commercial Conversion (CC - converting Commercial into residential). You can also JVs (Joint Ventures) with other property investors and/or loan money to people better qualified or more involved in specific investment strategies than you.

Buy To Sell (B2S)

You buy, ideally at a discount from market value, you refurb or do up the property to add value, and you sell, perhaps with some market growth, too. You take the big cash lump, pay your taxes and expenses and you pile your cash high. This is a lumpy, capital strategy that can fund other assets and is great for short-term gain but not so good for long-term passive income. In a rising market like we are currently in, this is an effective strategy.

When I got started in property I had no idea how to buy well or that you could indeed secure properties below market value (BMV). I educated myself on courses, found a business partner and bought my first BMV property in 2006. Within my first couple of years I had bought and sold 14 properties. The key to this success was to develop a system: the same kind of property, a refurbishment formula and a team to facilitate the sale. The mortgage market was quite a bit different then, and the now legendary "one day re-mortgage" from Mortgage Express was a key factor of the fast turnaround. I was making £5-15,000 in profit from every deal from a house below £125,000. Believe me, I was blown away by the profits in a short amount of time with limited experience. Things to consider here are capital gains tax from selling and the fact that you are not building an asset or creating cashflow from rentals. It's also a lesson that you have to "make hay while the sun shines," meaning taking opportunity while it presents itself. If a one-day re-mortgage product is offered (and it might be again in a few years) – know where you are in the property cycle of growth and recession and take advantage of it.

Buy To Let (B2L)

You buy, ideally at a discount, and you hold and rent out. Over time the asset grows in value, so you grow your asset and equity base, and you generate (mainly passive) income from rent minus costs.

You can do this with single lets, HMOs/multi-lets and commercial property (offices, industrial, retail, nursing homes). This is a great long-term strategy. If you buy enough below market value, there is a good chance that you can pull out most or all of your money on re-mortgage, currently a minimum of six months after the start of your mortgage.

I now hold a small portfolio of BTL properties. As most people do, I started out with buying one-bedroom leasehold flats. Looking back, I don't know why people do that! Yes, it's a lower threshold to get in, but it doesn't really make too much sense. Things to consider: you don't own the freehold, and management charges can be high (it's an unregulated market). Voids hurt, and small repairs will eat up your profit. Only consolation: your interest-only mortgage is being reduced by inflation as your asset increases in value. Yields (rental profits calculated from your cost of owning the property and getting it ready to let) are typically around 6-9 per cent. Profit can be set off against capital allowances to keep the property in a state where it can be let.

I learned about multi-lets a few years ago (HMO or house in multiple occupancy) and decided to buy some properties that leased themselves to be used as HMOs. They yield much higher than single lets, most of them in excess of 15 per cent (my top performer is 22 per cent). Things to consider: you can pull out extra money using commercial revaluations, where the lender lends to you based on the income from your property and not based on the bricks and mortar value. Make sure you find an agent that does room lets, as having 20 plus rooms can quickly turn into a job (you definitely don't want).

Commercial Conversion (Cc - To Rent Or Sell)
You buy a commercial property and either hold and rent out (like an office or a shop) or you convert into residential, utilising the

many tax and planning advantages currently available in the UK property market. A CC is a hybrid between investing and full- scale development, without the risk of development, by converting an existing building with commercial use and changing the use into residential, sometimes with full planning permission.

There is a chronic housing shortage in the UK, and the government can't solve it alone, so they give amazing tax and planning breaks to help you make profit and solve their long-term problems of housing shortages and empty office buildings dilapidating since the crash/ recession.

Rule number one in property: You make your money when you buy. Then you add value and you make more money. Voila. So being able to convert property allows you to add value in a bigger way.

I did my first small development by buying a house 100 per cent financed by a JV partner, for 10 per cent interest a year, and added a full extension, increasing the floor space, adding a room and an extra bathroom with planning permission.

The whole project was funded on credit cards, took eight months from purchase to sale and netted me £60,000. Things to consider: you could move into the property, make it your PPR (principal private residence) and then sell it without paying capital gains tax. I heard that HMRC are looking at people who do this serially, but there is no tax on gains from the property you're living in when you improve it. Check with your accountant for details - and this is NOT advice, just an FYI.

The second deal I want to mention is a conversion of a pub I bought in a JV. This project required around £400,000 in funding and will take about a year. What I love about it is that it has multiple angles to exploit. Firstly - the primary strategy is to go for planning and convert it into flats. With the precedent of planning in the area, it's a given. At the end of the project we'll be able to revalue the property and pull out all of the money that was required to do the deal. So in essence - no money in the deal equals free property. At this point we are expecting to also have about £400,000 in equity and £2-3,000 net positive cashflow from rent per month. Additionally there is a nice plot of land to the side that could either be sold off as a building plot or developed into a block of flats or houses. This is called a "big bonus" (official term). Things to consider: deals like this take more cash upfront but have a fantastic return. Because they are a little bit harder to do, there'll be less competition. Don't calculate your numbers on a best case or "all bonus strategies come off" scenario. Always be cautious with the costs and projected profits. Extra tip: have Mark Homer (co-founder of Progressive Property) as your JV partner.

Joint Venture (Jv) Or Loan

A JV (Joint Venture) is where two or more parties do a deal together. You use your cash and invest in a project with a partner who has the skills, experience and time to invest. You become the hands-free investor. Or the other way around where you do the work and your partner brings the cash to the table. In a JV, you own a share of the asset. In a loan you simply loan the partner the money for a fixed return.

Sometimes there is no deal that fits your criteria or strategy, so while you're waiting, your money sits in the bank being devalued by inflation and getting virtually no interest! That's not good. And because literally everyone runs out of cash at one point, JV's are a common way to keep people in the game. Sometimes I invest in other people's deals; sometimes they invest in my deals.

There are two ways to benefit from JVs. One is to loan your money for interest. 1-1.5 per cent a month is common, depending on how you secure it. Make sure you have a simple loan agreement and agree to a timeframe and what happens if you go beyond it. In essence you give them a secured or unsecured loan. Things to consider: you pay income tax on interest earned.

The second strategy is to go for a profit split in exit if it's a buy to sell deal or an equity and cashflow or cashflow and equity split if it's a buy-to-hold. The possible options are only limited by what the two parties are willing to agree to.

Things to consider: my tip is to keep it very simple. 50/50 is best, and make sure you talk about possible exit strategies for the parties as especially on buy-to-hold over the long term, one of you will have a different interest. The easiest way is to offer a first-refusal basis whereby the other party is being offered the share for a fair period of time before it is offered to the open market, based on the average of three independent valuations. Again, this is just what I've done - not necessarily what I advise you to do. Seek professional advice with all these - they are potentially long-term contracts with high stakes. But they are also very powerful aggregators for your long- term wealth.

The wealthy make huge amounts of money in property, and everyone in the Rich List has property, whether it is their main strategy like the Duke of Westminster, Earl Cadogan, Joseph Lau, Eddie and Sol Zakay, Andreas Panayiotou, James Caan or Lord Sugar, who made £48 million on a B2S in Central London. Or closer to home,

my multi-millionaire business and JV partners Rob Mooreand& Mark Homer, authors of five property books. If you want deep and specific knowledge of becoming a property multi-millionaire, I recommend you study them, as they are the best combination of doing it and teaching others how to do it in the UK today.

On top of that, property utilises leverage like no other asset I have ever seen or invested in and is right up there with public speaking and information marketing as the most leveraged cashflow strategy known to man.

Model 5. Stock Market

The stock market offers many packaged opportunities to leverage investment. You have passive investing strategies and you have trading strategies. You gain if a company grows in value through equity and dividend (according to your per cent ownership) or you lose in the other direction. You are hands- free, which can mean leverage of your personal time, but you can't control the outcome either.

First off, let's answer one of the most asked question in this cashflow strategy: Is there a difference between trading and spread betting? In one word, NO! In two words, YES and NO!

There's a common misconception that spread betting is more dangerous than trading, but the reality is that with the right system you can increase your returns by up to 40 per cent per year if you are a resident in the United Kingdom.

Whether you choose to spread bet or trade, there is no difference when it comes to executing your order. The difference comes when banking profits. And it can be large depending on your tax status.

You see, spread betting is, as the name suggests, classified as a form of gambling. This means that all winnings are tax-free in the UK. Trading returns are classed as a capital gain and therefore may be subject to tax. Of course, wherever tax is involved, your personal circumstances will certainly influence whether you need to declare the income from either variation to the tax authorities.

When you execute a trade, it is done electronically via an online platform. You can place exactly the same trade via a spread betting site or a trading platform. The only difference is whether you want to collect your winnings tax-free or whether you want to pay tax on your gains.

Using a tight rule-based methodology you can keep your risk the same but increase your returns by benefitting from the "tax exempt" status applied to gambling winnings. Why would you use a trading platform instead of a spreadbetting platform then? What I love most about trading is that it allows me to make money whilst I am.

My friend and Forex trading expert Dillon Dhanecha is consistently making a 1-3 per cent return a week (yes, a week, not a month or a year!) and gives away most of his profit to social enterprises. He is spending a lot of time travelling around the world visiting the projects that he supports.

When your trading account size grows to six figures or more, which it can do very quickly, then of course many other factors need to be considered, but when you get started you simply have to decide whether you wish to collect your winnings tax-free or declare tax on your gains.

Commodities/Shares Trading

Trading commodities (useful, tradable entities) or shares (in a company) is a simple value investing strategy where you buy at a good relative price and sell at a higher relative price. You can do this in two professional ways (as Wall Street or London Stock Exchange-type trading is very short-term and not recommended for long term profiting): good company, short-term problem.

You buy shares in a good long-term company that has a short-term problem and therefore offer a discount to the long-term value. Many people trade shares by buying into cheap stocks (remember penny stocks years ago) or start-up companies, or even companies with no proven income stream (remember the Internet stock bubble and bust around the year 2000).

Short-term, lucky cash can be made, but this won't last decades. Research a company that people need for the long term, has consistently returned equity growth and dividends to their shareholders and is not in a business than could change overnight or become outdated.

A recent example would be Tesco with claims of book cooking, resignations of the CEO and key staff and the stock market giving them a public beating. Though I am not recommending this investment, my business partners pound cost averaged (bought in stages) purchases in Tesco shares and have made a good return already as the short-term media attack began to die down and Tesco was able to assume business as usual.

It would be hard to imagine a High Street without a major supermarket, and now that Tesco sells virtually every product and has diversified into petrol, banking and insurance, it has a huge stronghold in the minds of anyone buying commodities for basic living.

You can look for companies that have decades of proven history that people need and are not exposed to change but are experiencing management or PR issues or are having legal or insurance claims that affect the short-term stock price.

Be patient, wait for the right company to experience a drop, pound cost average your purchase and sale of shares, and you may do well. But even the best will only get this right 50.8 per cent of the time, so you'd really want to do this for the long term and accept that you're going to get it wrong almost as often as you get it right.

This could just as easily be your buy and hold strategy, using the same concepts to buy in, but never selling, rolling up the dividend and not paying the tax on the profit made. Make sure you don't have to live off the proceeds from this strategy. It's long-term.

Two tips I took straight from no other than "me old mate Warren" (Buffet that is): "Never invest in a business you can't understand" and "It's far better to buy a wonderful company at a fair price than a fair company at a wonderful price."

Monopoly Business Investing:

Two big risks when investing in businesses are competition and market/legislation change. If you invest in a business that is in a competitive marketplace (through shares on the stock market), the company will at some stage get into a price war, and margins will thin over time, reducing your return.

The airline industry is a good example, and this is why you see so many airlines go bust. Because people price shop (they buy based mostly or wholly on price), the only advantage a company can get over its competitors is to drop the price to win market share or their loyalty programs. The only way they can do this is to reduce costs, and reducing costs thins profit, and you make your money through their profit. When a competitor makes the same savings they are able to compete with the company again on price, and they win back market share, and then the cycle continues.

In the 1960s it would cost $1,000 for an "around America" flight. It doesn't cost much more today, 55 years later, yet inflation has eroded most of that $1,000. Think how much lower the margin is now compared to the 1960s, and therefore how much lower the return on shareholders' equity is.

However if you invest in a company that has a (virtual) monopoly, where people need the product or service, you can maintain your margin because prices can rise with inflation and the customer will always buy through necessity. Find companies that hold the largest monopolies and study their trading history and you will see consistent returns over decades.

Can you imagine a shop surviving without selling Coca-Cola or Gillette? On a marketing trivia side note: Wilkinson, Gillette's closest competitor, has in independent tests been proven to have a better product. But who cares about the reality if Gillette's marketing slogan is, "The best a man can get!"

Not only do they have a monopoly on their markets, the stockists have to stock them or they wouldn't survive, so they have captive retailers, and they have repeat business through constant re-use. Coca-Cola doesn't just get used once in a lifetime; it gets used daily or more. Gillette sells you the product and then sells you the disposables, regularly. These companies not only have brand monopoly but you'll be going back to them daily, weekly, monthly for life. And the company can raise prices and you will keep using them, because you need them. Gillette's latest razor has now six blades! I remember when they brought out the one with two blades! Boy – I bet men back then were really badly shaven!

If you can buy their shares when they have a short-term problem, bad media or PR or a lawsuit of some kind, then you will buy in at a discounted price on future value, and you can sell out at a profit. Coca-Cola has for decades given investors an annual return of over 20 percent on shareholders' equity. Or you can continually reinvest the dividends, never sell and roll up the profit.

Passive Strategies:
You can break passive strategies into 3 main categories:

'Tracker' Investing:
Tracker investing is spreading your investments across a number of companies to reduce the risk of any one company going bust. You can do this safely through the FTSE 100 or 250 or the NYSE. You could also bypass an IFA's commissions for this by self-investing using Hargreaves Lansdown or another personal share trading/investing platforms. If trading is not your skill or legacy, you can still diversify your cash or assets and have a low-risk, hands-free element to your investment portfolio. Just don't expect huge returns, but at least you have relative security and liquidity.

Good Company, Short Term Problem:
The same as discussed earlier in this section but without the selling part. Buy and long-term hold, reinvest dividends to get a compounded return and protect from taxes.

Monopoly Business Investing:
The same as discussed earlier in this section but without the selling part. Buy and long-term hold, reinvest dividends to get a compounded return and protect from taxes.

I have learned from Warren Buffet on how to invest in stocks and shares for long-term profitability. I believe he is the best there is, and it is proven beyond doubt, hence why I chose him as my mentor. He was mentored by greats like Benjamin Graham and Charlie Munger. He did not get lured by short-term-ism such as the tech boom. He has quite a specific way of long- term "value investing," and you can pick up many books and audiobooks on his philosophy. He has managed to maintain an averaged 23 per cent a year return for more than six decades, and has turned $105 into more than $20 billion in his lifetime through his main investment company, Berkshire Hathaway.

Model 6. Low Risk Low Yield

I put all safe yet low-return investments that produce (low) income into this category. I'm by no means dismissing Low Risk Low Yield; as a balanced portfolio you should have low risk investments that are liquid. Low Risk Low Yield would include savings in the bank (as long as the interest rates can justify it), bonds from the government (low, fixed return but very safe), FTSE tracker type stocks and shares, physical assets such as gold or precious metals, watches that appreciate and ISAs.

Model 7. e-Commerce (Online resellers and member sites)

One of my favoured Income models is income from online sales. Electronic commerce, for short e-commerce, has been around for a good 20 years now, but only in the last few years been open to everyone. Previous to the democratisation of e-commerce, you needed many specialist skills and deep pockets to play in this market, and many players have had many years of losses before they made money. And many players of the early days have disappeared as the market consolidated. That is why now is such a great time to get involved. The first wave of the battle is over and you can back and partner with the clear winners.

E-commerce was called the $15 trillion gold rush by Forbes magazine in spring 2014 and Amazon, one of the biggest players in this space (25% of US e-commerce) have broken through the $100 billion turnover threshold looking to double it by 2017. That's not even mentioning Ebay or many of the other e-comm platforms you can use as a distribution and sales channel.

I was selling online for the first time back in 2006. At the time I worked a few badly paying jobs and selling as an affiliate (meaning selling someone else's product for commission) for pretty much no work was amazing. I got paid via cheques from America. Yes - ironically, Clickbank, still one of the largest digital marketplaces today, paid its affiliates in cheques. So I got US cheques every two weeks. He who's complaining. I remember my freshly opened USD account with HSBC crossing the $10,000 mark in disbelief!

In 2007 I applied and was granted the ability to sell online using a PayPal business account. I was officially now able to take money online. I remember distinctly the pleasure of waking up and having made money whilst I slept the night before (another fun part about selling in the US, from your laptop in the UK). The make-money-while-you-sleep attraction has still not lost its appeal! I make money in my pants when I sleep, I make money in my pants while doing webinars; in fact, making money in your clothes is so 1995.

In a lighter moment when brainstorming straplines for my business we also considered "Making money in my pants since 2006." Well, you guessed right. That didn't make it into the finals...

By 2008 I already made more than three times my job income and finally in 2009 I left my job. In 2009 I had membership sites with recurring income churning thousands of pounds a month and in 2010 I launched a new coaching programme with multiple upsells internationally. I made $250,000 in just 30 days, adding 871 customers from over 30 countries to my business. And I'd only quit my job less than a year before. It would have taken me 2,384 days to earn that in my Hewlett Packard job and 7,390 days as a pizza delivery boy. That's 20 years driving around Slough in a Skoda. Shiiiiit. I made most my money online selling information or information products. It's still a great market, although the value of digital information is definitely declining, and the Kindle has killed the e-book market. Back in 2007 we sold e-books (just a PDF) for $47 or even $97!

General e-commerce is complex, and if you want to sell physical products online you have the additional challenges of production, storage, distribution and other customer service-related issues. So when Amazon launched FBA (fulfilled by Amazon) a couple of years ago, which in essence means you deal with the marketing and they do the rest, it pretty much launched a new era of e-commerce. And I knew I wanted a part of it. Late in 2013 I started to sell physical products on Amazon, which has grown to a $500,000 business by the end of 2014. I love this business! It is exploding right now, the gold rush Forbes magazine talked about at the beginning of 2014. I'm expecting to do a minimum of $1 million by the end of 2015 – mainly automated and passive.

You see, in general you either have a cashflow business or an asset business. People love property because it can be both! And you can sell it based on the value of the asset.

It's the same here: An e-commerce business is mobile, scalable, can be systemised and it's easily sellable. And you are not just building a cashflowing business, you are building an asset that is based on the brand and the customer base you are building, which has a measurable value.

The Amazon business does not rely on me as a spokesperson or guru onstage having the skill to sell and market like a champ. It's a lot simpler and can be outsourced. My business partner James has pretty much outsourced everything about this business to various resources in the US and low-price economies. We pay our highly skilled workers in the Philippines less than $350 a month.

Model 8. Franchise And License (Physical)

A franchise (physical as opposed to IP) is authorisation granted by a company to commercialise a process or business model in exchange for fees (capital) and residual profit share (income). A franchise is a license to follow a system of business created by someone else (or a company), and create a profitable branch of that business, paying a fee and splitting the profit.

The franchise model is proven, and if you are the franchisee (the license holder or purchaser) you are investing in a proven process, thereby reducing the risk of start-up capital and high chances of failure. You follow the manual created by the franchisor and you increase your chances of success. The franchisor gets a fee for the start up (capital) and a residual share of profits, in exchange for the system, model and on-going training.

Common franchises are Subway, Pizza Hut, KFC, ReMax, Hertz, Marriott, Golds Gym and Cartridge World. Notice that all of them are based on reusable or recurring goods or services.

You could look at franchising from both angles: being the franchisor (owner) or franchisee (purchaser). My business partner Rob Moore has a property networking franchise, Progressive Property Network. They are currently pushing 40 PPNs in the UK. The fee is just £9,000 a year for a minimum three-year term, there is a small management fee, and then ticket and course sales revenues are shared between franchisee and franchisor. If a franchise venture is successful then it makes money for both parties, and ideally the income is residual through regular use and consumption.

If you have been in business a long time or have a special process, system or piece of software, or just make a usually hard model simple, then you could franchise your IP or system. You have all the knowledge in your head. You may even have an existing brand with goodwill, so the icing on the cake is to create or leverage more capital and income from what you've already done. It may take you one extra year or low tens of thousands of pounds, and you could license what you already have to create a scalable franchise model and manual.

This is common in fast food, cleaning, car rental, lettings, estate agencies, ink cartridges, coaching and training businesses, sign writing, even donuts and sweetcorn! Yes franchises take management, but you are getting both capital and income in franchising, and you might be building equity in selling the entire business in the future.

The license part or model of a franchise is simply where you rent the name of a brand. I was waking round the Emirate Mall in Dubai today and noticed many licensed brand names, like Hugo Boss, who license their name to companies who create aftershave; a joint venture where Hugo Boss leverages the fragrance company and the fragrance company leverages the Hugo Boss brand. Or if you own a sky scraper in the US, you could consider licensing the 'trump' name for your building – it'll cost you a minimum of $10m, but – if you fit the criteria – could add tens of millions of value to your bricks and mortar value. Celebrities license their name to products, restaurants and so on and generate a big revenue stream. Leverage for both parties and the power and value of building a personal brand around your expertise.

It's not for $10 million, but I have licensed the IP and trainings of my Expert Success Formula to a German license partner. Licenses are a lot less regulated than franchises, and in this particular license agreement the master licensee has the right to sell my workshops and trainings and use my IP and I get 50 per cent of the profit after deduction of reasonable expenses (to avoid the temptation of draining profits with high cost). A second level of the license agreement allows the master licensee to sell coaching licenses to disseminate the knowledge.

Model 9. Physical Business

The most common type of business is, well, a business. Before many of the innovations we've discussed and the leverage the Internet has brought, it was common to set up premises, invest in stock, plant and machinery, human capital (staff) and start producing and selling. Farming, industrial, merchandising, etc. are almost "old-school" now, but that certainly doesn't mean you should overlook them. In fact these businesses are often heritage or monopoly businesses and therefore virtually unbreakable. And if you look down the rich list, many of the top positions are held by families you've never heard of running businesses in manufacturing or other industries.

The start-up costs and risks are lower today but still very high compared to online businesses or service-based businesses, but the rewards for a physical business are potentially greater than every model here, because you utilise virtually every capital and income stream. You turnover sales, you create profits after fixed and variable costs, you build equity through either owning the premises or building equity value in the business itself, or both. You can employ yourself and pay yourself a salary, you can draw dividends or drawings (structure dependent) as income, and you can gain efficient tax breaks through trading and corporate structuring. Sweet.

There was a little craze in the 2000s where the dream was to live on a boat with a laptop and work anywhere in the world and have no staff, but the reality is that all wealthy people have "real" businesses. Business is what generates capital. Fees are paid in lumps or stages, and those revenues are distributed among staff, consultants, suppliers, the Inland Revenue (or IRS in the US), cleaners, gardeners and retainers such as HR and IT; virtually everyone in your local and macro economy is benefitting from your business enterprise. As long as you are getting your fair share, then it's a win-win. And this is what drives the economy. Boom!

As long as there is demand for the product or service and you can meet the demand with supply, there is fair exchange, and you can make a margin by buying lower that you sell (minus expenses), then free enterprise is born.

The longer you own your business (and manage it well), the higher the capital value it will retain. You will have assets on the balance sheet (that could include the previously mentioned IP), you will have cash in the bank, you will have trading and operational history proven by certified accounts, you will have brand goodwill, invoices (debtors), and all of this will create capital value that you could wholly sell or sell shares in (through an IPO).

If you look at your business legacy in retained value terms and have a long-term view of your business serving your own legacy through purpose, you will almost by default create huge capital value without trying. It's like making vast equity in a house accidentally that you only intended to live in. An individual or company could pay you a price/earnings ratio or EBITDA (Earnings before interest, tax, depreciation and amortization) for your business that could work out multiples of turnover or profit. A friend of my business partners sold his tech company in the year 2000 for 39 times turnover! $1 billion in the bank.

Summary

Capital and income (cashflow) are required to fund your desired lifestyle and live your legacy. It forms a large part of your Wealth DNA and is the physical manifestation of success and living your purpose. Creating flow to you and through you is, like anything, a learned skill and system. You can influence and manipulate the flow towards yourself to enrich and enable you to do more of what you want, when you want, with whoever you want (if you're lucky), wherever you want. Money doesn't make you happy, but money doesn't make you unhappy, either; it is simply a physical form and mechanism of exchange and only has the meaning that you project onto it based on your values and beliefs (that you can influence and change). Wealth is about freedom to live your legacy through purpose, self-funded through assets kicking out passive income. Yeah!

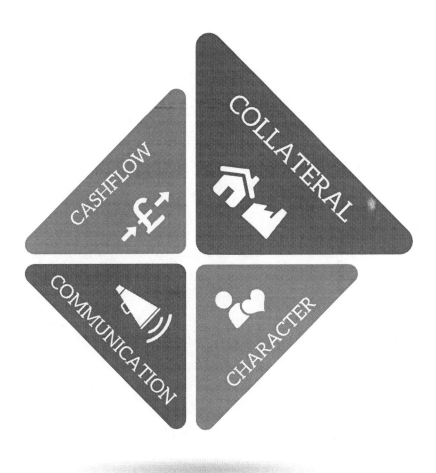

The Wealth Diamond: The 2nd C – Collateral

The 2nd C in the Wealth Diamond is collateral. Collateral is your leverage and security. It's what you bring to the table. Collateral is the tangible and intangible asset that backs an investment, idea, contract, promise or commitment. It is your guarantee, your reputational promise that you will deliver and the risk reduction of working with you.

129

The Oxford Dictionary defines it as "something pledged as security for repayment of a loan, to be forfeited in the event of a default" (thanks, Oxford Dudes, helpful as always). The intangible collateral is what others say about you, your brand, reputation, word and goodwill. It is what people will pay a license fee for. It is how many times you have delivered on your promise and your proof through the voices and recommendations of others. It is the security that an investment in you will pay a dividend, or an asset can be called in, in return.

I recently promoted an online training course as an affiliate, meaning I sent a recommendation to my list and asked them to invest in the product. Not only did we make $1 million in sales in just nine days, we also had the lowest refund rate across the world from dozens of promoters. Why? Well it was partly the trust and goodwill – intangible collateral that I called in over those nine days.

Without collateral, banks won't lend you money, customers won't believe your big claim or promise, staff won't work for you 30 days in arrears, your children won't trust in what you ask them to do, start-ups won't start up, mortgages won't be given for houses, contractors won't work to invoice terms, car hire firms won't hire cars to you and those you've fallen in love with won't go out on a date with you. It's what you bring to the table to engage in life.

One of the six human needs according to Tony Robbins is certainty; human beings are constantly seeking certainty and want to avoid pain. In business it's normally called risk (also manifests as losses, mistakes, pain, embarrassment, looking like an idiot... you get the picture). Anything that can increase certainty, even guarantee it, and therefore de-risk, will make the (any) decision easier and therefore promote transaction and speed up business growth.

Before I'll talk more about collateral and the two main categories it can be broken down to, let me share a concept with you that I find hugely fascinating – I call it the 10x Challenge.

The 10x Challenge

Between 2007 and 2014 I did what I now call 10x. I created a ten-fold increase in my pay, I multiplied my value by 10 in the marketplace. In other words, I got a 1,000 per cent pay rise. That is only possible if you work for yourself from my experience and by changing your Wealth DNA and using and applying some of what I share in this book.

How would it work out if you went to your boss on Monday and asked for a pay rise? And not just a few per cent (below the real inflation in most cases by the way) but for a proper pay rise – like double or triple. Or 1,000 per cent. Well you can kind of predict what would happen – right?

But the question you should be asking yourself is, What could you do to increase your value in the marketplace by 1,000 per cent? What could you do that pays ten times what you earn right now? And I know that it is hard to imagine, but if you control the asset, the collateral, the business, why not? And it's worthwhile letting your brain come up with answers – because it is of course possible to multiply your value and therefor multiply your income.

I remember living in the cubicle in my job at HP as a trainer. And every office has a ... let's call them a difficult person. It's the much-loved topic of office politics. The guy I remember in my office was called Rudi from Belgium. He was just a guy you wanted to avoid, and I'm sure everyone works with or remembers their own Rudi. If you work for yourself, a lot of these problems will go away.

But forget Rudi – forget the hours wasted at the water cooler or the days wasted on meetings about nothing or the days creating reports for different levels of management... What I hated the most about my job at HP was that on the first of January I pretty much knew how much I would have earned by the end of the year no matter how dedicated or hard I worked or what I did or how much effort I put in.

If what you do and your effort is not directly linked to how much you make – that is depressing in my eyes. And when you have to write a 20-page appraisal to apply for a 3 per cent pay rise, that's not just humiliating, it's a joke! Because with real inflation (not the number they publish in the media as a Retail Price Index) being a minimum of 7 per cent, you are actually applying for 4 per cent pay decrease! And it was the same year HP laid off 60,000 people to satisfy shareholder expectations.

I definitely wasn't in control. The whole idea of creating your own plan and changing your Wealth DNA is to get back in the driving seat. Now that didn't happen overnight for me, but it started with a decision that just took seconds!

You need a plan. I only quit my job in January 2009. I was already making a decent income (multiples of my salary) from other income streams. I'm a cautious person. I'm not a big risk taker. We all have different risk profiles, and you create your own plan – but you have to get started with reducing your dependency on earned income and replace it as fast as you can with leveraged income.

Now, let me ask you, and this is a very important question: if you wanted to do 10x... if you wanted to earn or turnover ten times what you earn right now... What would you have to do? Let's say you are earning £28,000 a year. Who would you have to become to demand £280,000 a year?

Most likely your mind's gonna go blank. No clue? And that makes sense. How would you know?

Most of you can't say, "I just work 10 times as hard or work 10 times as many hours." That's the problem with the time-for-money model. So, you have to become resourceful and ask yourself, What can I bring to the marketplace that can get me 10 times the income? How can I create 10 times the value?

This is what I call the 10x Challenge. And that's why the 10x Challenge is part of the second C of the Wealth Diamond. Because you have to have more collateral! First off, you have to find out if there is indeed anyone in the world doing what you do or in your field that earns or makes 10x of what you currently do. If yes, great news. So even if you don't know how, someone knows. So go find them and pay them to help you get there.

If you're a coach, trainer, consultant or speaker, then you can get my book Expert Success from Amazon. It outlines positioning strategies to help you increase and even multiply your turnover and profit. It's not my focus anymore, but for years I ran workshops and training programs on how to become a highly paid expert, and many of my clients have experienced the 10x Effect.

One thing is certain, though. Whatever it is you'll have to do or who you will have to become to attract 10 times the money will be way outside your current comfort zone.

One of my mentors once said, "Your Comfort Zone equals your Income Zone." So if you want to expand what you're earning, you got to expand what you are comfortable doing. It's all about learning the next level skills. And they exist, but they exist outside your world of comfort and normality. For example the property development deal I'm doing right now is a new level of investment and skill, and I'll be straight with you: it's outside my Comfort Zone. But I know it will take me to the next level Income Zone. And I already know that at the end of it I'll be comfortable with this kind of investment and will push on to the next level. And the next level means more cash, baby!

If it's possible, I'll do it. I know I have the response-ability to deal with the challenge. And so do you, my friend.

That's the 10x Challenge for me right now. And for you? It's the same question but with a different answer.

The 10 X Challenge
Wealth DNA

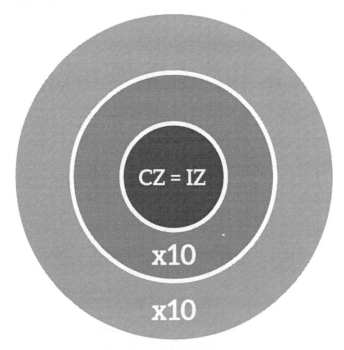

Tangible Collateral (Assets):

Tangible Assets come in the form of:
- Property
- Stock
- Plant & machinery
- Debtors
- Human
- Other physical Assets

Property
Property is almost universally recognised as the best form of collateral, or security. It has proven to be the most stable and appreciating asset class and has extended utility over centuries. It is the single asset we cannot do without, and therefore we will ensure we protect at all costs from default, therefore acting as great security for lenders, insuring their investment is safe and will be paid back.

A bank will lend with a charge against a buy to let, commercial or residential property. A JV partner can use equity in your property as security for a loan by way of second charge, restriction or loan agreement. The saying "safe as houses" is so for a reason.

Security
Security is the default control or protection given (away) against an asset in case of default. Security can come in many forms such as a charge, restriction, covenant, contract, loan, power of attorney, share agreement, partnership agreement or personal guarantee. The riskier the investment, the more onerous the security needed will be. Be prepared to give security when investing or borrowing money. Just be careful not to give personal guarantees for new or risky investments.

Stock

Stock is physical inventory held in advance of sales. Stock is an asset in that it has cash tied up for future sales, but can also be a liability for cashflow or lack of liquidity and wastage. Stock will be on the balance sheet and can be used as collateral in the selling or raising finance for a business, or for future cashflow projections or sales. It is a much riskier form of collateral than property and also has storage or degradation implications, which is why a bank won't put a charge against your stash of underwear or vinyl collection for a loan.

Plant and Machinery

Much like stock, plant and machinery will be on the balance sheet (depreciated) as an asset and has very similar properties. There is the added implication of maintenance, especially in manufacturing, technology and industrial.

Debtors

Debtors are outstanding invoices to be paid to you or your company, loans or money owed. Debtors can be in the form of one-time transactions or clients, but also in the form or recurring billings (such as tenants to a letting agency or recurring monthly memberships).

Companies with residual debtors have a higher P/E or EBITDA valuation because the guarantee of future money is higher, and therefore the risk of investing is lower. It will make a more attractive proposition for investors investing into your business, or for selling your business in the future, thereby acting as collateral for a higher valuation.

There is also invoice factoring where you can borrow short-term money against longer-term outstanding invoices, giving them asset and collateral value.

Human

Human collateral is quite possibly the most leverageable of all collateral. Human collateral comes in the form of staff, network and friendships. Human collateral is the leverage you have in other people assisting you to your legacy through purpose. It is how many people work for you, follow your lead and vision, and utilise their time and expertise in collaboration with you. It is the favours you can call in and the goodwill you own in other people.

It is how Warren Buffett and Bill Gates created $100 billion empires, because they certainly couldn't have done that on their own! They achieved vast fortunes with tens of thousands of staff members and leveraging the success of companies with, in turn, tens of thousands of staff. And they self-fulfilled the legacy by building the reputation that attracted more of the same. The level of leverage from human collateral depends on legacy and influence, both covered in this book.

Other Physical Assets

You may be able to use other physical assets as collateral, such as precious metals. People often make guarantees in bets as a form of collateral. It's high risk, but it's only a lack of creativity that limits your collateral leverage. You could contract services, offering a service as collateral for a service. Loan notes, SPVs (Special Purpose Vehicles) and all sorts are used as collateral.

Intangible Collateral (Assets):

Intangible Assets come in the form of:
- IP (Franchise)
- Brand, reputation & goodwill
- Promise & guarantee
- Recommendations & referrals

IP (Franchises & Licenses)

IP acts as intangible collateral in the form of a promise, system or software. An idea can be patented, and that ownership can attract capital to grow a business.

Customers, franchisees and licensees will invest money and pay fees and shares of profits in the idea or unique system, leveraging your experience and process collateral. The brand and experience behind the IP or franchise acts as security collateral, reducing the start-up risk to the franchisee. The franchise system or license to use IP becomes the asset that is collateral for the recurring income. The brand and proof collateral is what makes the franchisee work hard to make the income that the franchisor gets a share of.

Brand, Reputation & Goodwill

Brand (personal brand, corporate identity, reputation and goodwill), reputation and goodwill all act as collateral in an intangible marketing form. They all form "mindspace," a small owned neurological pathway in the mind of an individual that is processed unconsciously and instantly to trigger a "Yes I trust you" or "No way, Jose!" response.

In essence you want to own the neural pathway – or simply the thought connection between a commodity, product or service and your company or name. If I say "fast food chain," what are you thinking?

It'll be pretty much the same thought everyone else has. Because the big "M" has spent countless millions and many decades linking their brand with a range of products and services. If I said "running shoes," who owns that space in your mind? Chances are it's Nike or Adidas. They have again spent a lot of money and time to own that neural pathway.

Corporations spend billions to own that little space in someone's mind, when someone becomes hungry or needs a new computer or phone or pair of trainers or golf clubs or face cream.

This is not just relevant for corporations who can spend billions. It's the same in any area. If I say "wealth education," I want to be the connection firing in your brain.

This culminates in trust and makes influence and decisions easy and fast. It might be intangible, but it is very powerful and as important as the physical manifestation it creates. Guard this with your life and be strategic about the messages you are sending out. Act like everyone is watching all the time, stay truthful and don't do anything that conflicts with your values and beliefs. Invest as heavily in the intangible as you do in the tangible.

Promise & Guarantee

Your promise is the big claim that you or your product or service makes, that you are required to live up to upon delivery. The guarantee is the reduction of risk and the certainty of the big claim being the reality, after the investment. Some of this is given (you expect a coffee to be hot, fruit to be ripe and sweet and a taxi to get you to your destination) and some of this is "nice to have." The key to promise and guarantee is to be bold enough to make the big claim, match it with a ballsy guarantee to reduce the risk, then not only live up to it but to over deliver. If you meet these criteria, then your brand, reputation and goodwill will soar and you will attract people from all over the globe to become part of your legacy through purpose. You will create such strong brand loyalty that people will never leave you, constantly recommend you and queue up for hours or days to see you. This will then lead to a constant stream of effortless recommendations and referrals.

Recommendations & Referrals

When you live according to the rules of this book and write your own Wealth DNA through your highest values and legacy, you will magnetically pull customers, followers and raving fans from all across the globe to you.

Recommendations and referrals are the final manifested reality that you are living true to your highest order and purpose, in the state of flow and unique greatness that is radiant, attractive and inspiring to others. Yes, you can ask for recommendations and referrals. Yes, you can buy them through affiliations, but you can't grow them and pull them magnetically unless you are living true to your purpose and changing your Wealth DNA.

Summary

Collateral is the guarantee and security you and your assets offer to attract finance, customers and goodwill. Without collateral, there is no backing for the income or the customer, and so it won't stick with you. It is the foundation of a building, the guardian of an overseas child and the guarantor of a university student's rent. It is the hidden magnet that makes promises, pitches and offerings plausible and believable and less risky and scalable. It might not be as sexy as cashflow, but it is as integral as cashflow in the 4 Cs and often overlooked. It is the silent assassin and the hidden gem.

The Wealth Diamond:
The 3rd C – Character

The third C in the Wealth Diamond is character. Your character is what is unique, charismatic, attractive and inspiring about you, in intangible asset form. Your character is your legacy through purpose shining outwards. It is your ability to live your legacy through purpose with conviction, strength and compassion. It is the essence of both who you are and who you were meant to be. Just as a diamond is simply carbon transformed under pressure in the right environment, your character is formed through the same trials, tribulations, rejections and victories that every other person on the planet experiences, but in your unique expression it will shine like a diamond, attractive, valuable and lasting.

The expression of your Character can be seen in 3 parts:
1.   In your Leadership
2.   In your Mindset
3.   In your Network

Leadership

Being a leader is a responsibility and an honour that you should take seriously. Your legacy through purpose cannot be achieved on your own, so you will need to lead people to assist you in your purpose. You may need hundreds, thousands or even millions of people to serve your purpose, and leadership will take three main characteristics: courage, vision and the power of influence.

Most people do not have the courage, vision or influence to lead, though everyone could in an area of their highest purpose. Because following a leader is safer, less risky and more secure, many people will settle below their purpose and be led or influenced by people in positions of authority, social proof or high rank. Your role in the character part of the four Cs of your Wealth DNA is to tune in to your legacy and become the person you need to be to lead and inspire.

Courage

Courage in most occasions is not superhuman, saving people from burning houses or leaping from a bridge into three feet of water. Courage is the ability to be human, to be vulnerable, to get rejected, to make mistakes, to look silly in front of others and to be able to embrace the gifts and learn in it; to laugh it off even. And importantly to learn and grow from it. It's not about trying to avoid mistakes, but to be open to the lessons from them and move on. To be ready to grow and learn to expand your comfort zone.

Courage is not about being stronger, fitter, faster or more gifted. It is not about performing miracles of bravery; these are simply excuses others project so they don't have to tackle challenging tasks; most notably to the ego. Human beings perform acts of courage every second of every day, when believing in something or living through purpose. So it is legacy and living through purpose that inspires everyday courage, which simply means that you will try and you may fail. Most won't die, yet many inspiring leaders have lived so much through purpose that they died for their legacy, only to make it stronger. Just to make this clear – you will (most likely) not have to die for your cause or legacy.

You know through personal experience that success is sweeter when it is hard to obtain. You know you learned the most in your failures not your easy wins. You know you built your character around challenge and hardship, and although you may not have enjoyed it at the time, it made you who you are. And you are unique and amazing as you are. So simply remember this and know that you have courage in-built, when the task or obstacle is new or scary to you. What is now easy was once hard, and every master was once a disaster.

Vision

I have not talked about vision much in this book yet, because I see legacy as the end goal of the vision and purpose as your way of living it. Vision is really about giving people hope. Without hope we are dead, even if we are alive. Without hope we have nothing to live for, so hope is the fuel that keeps us alive.

Vision is helping someone else see a future through you and your legacy through purpose. It is giving them hope that they can be, do and have whatever they want, through your leadership, utopia or better, different, unique path.

Vision is not about being able to see where you want go, what you want to be, do and have; it is about communicating it to others so they can see it and, importantly, see themselves in it. Once they see it, then they need to believe they can be a part of it or can achieve it, and then you lead them towards it. Once the why and the what is clear, the how will be easy.

Influence

Influence is your ability to change someone's mind or vision or perception, and to redirect their path towards yours. Here is my definition of influence, which I adapted from my business partner Rob Moore's: Influence is "leading someone to do what you know is good for them, having them believe it was their decision and then thanking you for it."

Influence is not manipulation or gimmicky trickery for short-term gain, for that will create remorse, resistance and ultimately rebellion. Influence is living legacy through purpose with conviction and authenticity, so that you don't fear rejection, mistakes or embarrassment when leading others. Influence is mindspace, brand, personal power, what strangers think of you, reputation, communication, resilience and charisma, confidence and concern for other people. Influence is trust that you have the best interests of the person in mind, and allowing them to make the right decision with your guidance.

The way I see it, we all influence each other all the time. And the person with the clearer vision and stronger conviction and more energy will win, every time. I mentioned earlier that you either have your own plan or you're part of someone else's plan. Lead or be led. Influence or be influenced.

If you have anything you believe is worth pursuing, you'll need people to be part of it, as your team, as your clients, as your support. You will need to influence their thinking and their behaviour and so it's a skill you must pursue and aim to master.

Mindset

Your mindset, or psychology, is how you think and how you make decisions based on how you feel and react to situations that arise in everyday life. These in turn are based on who you are and what you hold to be true and important. You will react in any given situation positively or negatively based on your truths and what you hold most important in your life; so mindset isn't just about 'being positive', it's about changing and tuning how you react to the world based on who you are to serve your purpose.

In order to change and improve your mindset habitually and for the long-term, we need to go deeper and discover our identity, values and beliefs. Identity; who you are. Values; what is most important to you in your life. Beliefs; your truths and realities that you hold with conviction.

Identity

If you want to change the fruits, you have to change the roots, so going deep into who we are is the most powerful place for mindset shifts. After all, if it were superficial and easy, you'd stop eating ice cream and pizza now (you know it's bad for you!), you'd jump up at 6 A.M. with energy and do your Yoga now, you'd control anger, envy, jealousy, guilt and shame now and all the other things you know are not good for you but still in some way support you. It's not that simple! If success were easy, everyone would be doing it, right?

In order to know your identity, simply answer the question:

'Who am I?'

Who are you? Have you ever really thought about that properly?

'Who am I?'

Who you are drives everything in your life, so it is well worth some time to think about. Funny that at school you learned how to light magnesium with a Bunsen burner, you learned how to ask how to get to the library in French, you learned Pythagoras's theory, but you were never asked the question, "Who are you?" Take some time now to think about these:

'Who am I?'

'What do I stand for?'

'What will I not tolerate?'

'How do I want to be known?'

'How do I want to be remembered?

You might take as much time as you like to yourself to answer this question. Write it down and make sure you can access it on all your devices and keep a track/history of your notes (for example, on an app like Evernote). Ask your friends and loved ones this question and let them talk openly and honestly. Collate your findings and distil it into a short paragraph or couple of sentences. It will not be the definitive answer to the human condition, but a snapshot of how you are in the world as you see it. And it will (and has to) change as you change your Wealth DNA.

Values

Once you have considered who you are, consider the question:

"What is most important to me in my life?"

Your values are simply the things that are most important to you, the areas of your life you feel alive living. Values are short words or phrases, such as health, family, wealth, security, or adventure. They come from your parents, your society (culture, geography, community), media influences, friends and family, peer group and network, schools/universities, what you read/learn, the mentors you have – anyone or thing that impressions or forms you. Some of them come from the depth and core of your humanity.

As conscious or unconscious as you might be about these values, you live your life according to these, experience results according to these (and failures), experience order according to these (and chaos) and experience joy according to these (and sadness, frustration, anger). What you hold as most important you will spend most of your time on and therefore create order in, and the polar opposite you will ignore and therefore experience chaos or disorder in.

This is why they are worth examining and this is why you may want to re-prioritise them.

If you are a parent and spend all your time with your kids you will have results and connection in that area, but you may not earn much money. If you spend all your life at work, you might have a great career but your relationship may die. You might travel lots and have freedom but struggle to hold down a relationship or home or your health might suffer. The "Wheel of Life" exercise that I explained at the beginning of this book simply highlights what you value most. How else would you have made the decision to focus on certain areas over others?

One of the sad things about life is that most people are living in an hypnotised daze where they have no idea consciously how they live their life, what is most important to them and why they are doing what they are doing in any given moment. They simply react to their thoughts that they have no control over, they are a victim to ingrained habits and auto- responses and they have no control over how they feel, what they do or the results they get. They are in many aspects like machines.

In this next section you will learn what I believe should be mandatory in schools. You will discover that you can choose to live your life in an awakened state where you have full control over your actions, reactions, behaviours and results. You will know exactly why you react a certain way, and you will be able to change what you don't like about how you fact to situations. You will discover exactly why you are succeeding in some areas of your life and failing in others (though the reality is that you are succeeding in every area of your life according to your focus which is driven by your values).

Here we go...

Answer this question in the form of a brief list of words of very short phrases:

'What is most important to you in your life?'

List between five and ten words and try not to overthink it; simply let them flow out in the order and speed at which they want to most naturally. Go. Do it now.

OK – if you are one of the people who don't like to do exercises while you read or just say "I'll do it later," then I'm fine with that. Just promise me now you'll get back to this one, because it's good for you, OK? Just mark the page or something and don't forget (or to use my NLP knowledge – do remember!).

Now that you have done that and written your values down, have a look at them. This simple list in front of you is your life. It is how you live it, how you spend your time, how you fill your space, where you spend most of your time and with whom.

Based on the influencing factors listed earlier in this section, your life value has been formed, moulded and evolved. Some things have been there for many years, some have recently changed due to significant emotional events in your life, but all are who you are. So the big question is:

"Is this who you want to be?"

Do your values look like you want them to according to your legacy? Do the areas at the top (most important) reflect where you want order, success and happiness? Are there significant values missing in this list that could explain why you are attracting chaos, dysfunction and unhappiness in that area of your life? This is who you are, but is it who you want to become?

Your current Wealth DNA is formed by these values, and importantly based on where wealth, money, business, success or career is on your values list. (If they are not there at all – I can guess how well you're doing in these areas!) Whatever word or short phrase you used to represent wealth (as it is personal to you and defined by you) is appearing (or not appearing) on the list relative to your successes (high) or failures (low), order (high) or chaos (low). So the big question for this book is:

"Where is Wealth on your values list?"

If it is middle to low or non-existent, there is the answer staring you in the face as to why you haven't attracted or manifested wealth into your life. Because it hasn't been (unconsciously or consciously) important enough to you, so you have not focused on it as much as you have all the values that are higher in the list. And because you haven't focused on it, your results have been accidental or circumstantial, not strategic.

So if you are one of the people who have not done the exercise (and hey – I can relate) maybe you want to do it now?

If, as you look at your list, wealth (or whatever words describes that to you) is high on the list but you feel lacks results or order, then either you "doctored" the list (unconsciously – after all, you are reading a book on wealth) or it has recently moved because you have started to focus on it (after all, you are reading a book on wealth) and therefore it is higher through current focus and importance, but the results are in "lag," because it hasn't been there for long.

Your next, most powerful exercise is to re-order your values and begin the process of living your life through legacy consciously and strategically. Have a look at your values list and answer this question:

"Who Do I Want To Be And Become?"

Move up what you feel needs to be more important and more of a focus in your life, and let those not so important naturally drop. Look at how much higher wealth needs to be and what else needs to be higher relative to it to live out your legacy. If family and health have been affected by career or travel you can move them up, if everything has been affected by a (lack of) wealth, then move that right up there; go on, I dare you. Of course I am not saying by writing a list and then re-writing it will pull in a cheque from my bank account to you for a seven-figure sum hand-delivered with a bow and compliment slip, but this where it has to start. The conscious process of starting to live your ideal life.

You can create three to five options of your list, and then spend time looking at them and letting them process in your unconscious mind before picking your "final" (at this moment in time) list.

Read your values each morning as soon as you get up to start your day with volition and purpose, and read them as you drift off to sleep to let your subconscious mind go to work to manifest them.

Beliefs

Now that you know your identity and values, from there your beliefs are driven and formed. Your beliefs are what you hold to be true with conviction. They are your moral and ethical codes, they are what you stand for and against, they are what you would fight for, argue over and in some cases even kill for. When you change (or become consciously aware of) your identity and values, your beliefs, including your money beliefs and Wealth DNA, are formed and changed.

For example if "giving" has moved up your values list, then what you believe about money and what you should do with it will automatically change. The actions and results will then manifest in your life accordingly. Your beliefs are linked to your legacy living through purpose; they create your rights and wrongs, your energy and inspiration and commitment to a cause.

The next stage in the third C, character, is to look at your wealth and money beliefs.

"What do you hold true around Wealth?"

"What do you stand for and against?"

"What is your moral and ethical code?

And therefore

"What results are you manifesting around Wealth?"

I'm sure you can now start to see how your beliefs are the roots that are bearing the fruits of your wealth, whether they are a vineyard of fat, juicy grapes or a single shrivelled raisin. I will tell you story about wealth beliefs close to home for me and then I will list wealth vs. poverty beliefs that are polarised but manifest results accordingly.

How A Warped Money Belief Has Kept Me Broke

I wondered for a long time why, despite my efforts, wealth eluded me. I worked hard, I was a good man, yet money seemed to flow away from me, and the harder I chased, the faster it got away.

I was determined, though, to find out what was going on. I went to seminars about money mindset, I spoke to friends, I went to therapy. I somehow knew that there was some underlying, unconscious belief that held me back.

One late Saturday evening in July 2008 I had my much-desired breakthrough. I was in America at the time in the middle of a transformation process when I was able to connect the dots. Information I knew suddenly became a story, and the story made sense. It explained why I had this fear of money and how it had so powerfully kept me broke.

It wasn't the only belief, it wasn't the only thing that had held me back, and it still took some time to manifest the new beliefs, but it was the pivotal moment in changing my Wealth DNA.

It might come as no surprise that the answer to my problem was buried deep inside my family. I haven't told you much about me or my family, but at this stage in the book I will, as it is relevant to understand how powerful beliefs can be to help you or hinder you from getting what you want.

I grew up in an apartment in a tower block in a small town in Austria (hence my funny writing style that I asked my editors not to edit out). My dad had a decent job, and our family was pretty much like most other families in the block. Married parents with two kids, mum at home, standard Austrian family in the 1970s.

We were not broke but also had no money, apart from the salary of my dad. I remember that businesspeople were somehow envied and wealthy people were never part of our family's network. Dad drove an average car, and we went on two-week holidays every year to Italy by car.

I will save my teenage years through drug addiction and the rest of it for another day, but what is relevant is that I desired wealth from a very young age and had a liking for selling and business, which my mum attributed to having Jewish blood. Mum's dad was Jewish, but I never met him or knew much about him.

My life in the spiritual group was uneventful, and I was broke and afraid to do what I really wanted, but I still desired wealth very much.

I must have been in my thirties when I learned more about my background. Mum one day told me that my grandfather had been a very successful and wealthy businessman, and that she had lived around money until the age of seven. The largest shopping centre in Innsbruck (my hometown) was part owned by my grandfather. He had over eighty employees, and my mum lived in the penthouse top floor of the shopping centre, in the city centre.

That was until 1938. Pretty much overnight the Germans had annexed Austria, and soldiers outside my grandfather's store had painted the Star of David on the shop windows. They'd smeared "Don't buy from Jews" on it and blocked people from going in. Within a few months he was forced to sell.

There is lot more to the story, of course, and the many years of painful unsuccessful attempts to get the family back what was stolen from them is just one aspect of it, but what is more important is that my mum, aged seven, had somehow created the belief that if you have money, they will come after you and take it from you.

Even worse, some of my relatives died in concentration camps. My grandfather went to Palestine, which became Israel in 1948, and never came back. I read some of his diary of the last few months in

Innsbruck, and it's chilling. It is one of the reasons why I don't live in Austria and why I came to England.

England is the country that gave my mum refuge. She was seven when she was put on the Kindertransport organised by the Quakers. She loved England all her life for it. And so do I.

Although my mum never consciously passed on these beliefs to me, do you think it's possible that the beliefs were woven into our upbringing? The fear of having everything taken away from you? Including your parents. Would you choose a humble existence and tell your kids to do the same just to be on the safe side? Of course.

So that late Saturday in 2008 I connected the dots. I understood that much of my failure to attract and acquire wealth and my self-sabotage around money was based in my mother's childhood experience. There were tears. Tears of pain, tears of regret but also tears of relief and tears of joy. I knew that day that the spell was broken.

And within a few short years literally my whole Wealth DNA had changed. From money repellent I turned into a money magnet.

I have since discovered other little gremlins that have hindered my progress, and I'm working on eradicating them, but my question to you is this:

Do you think it's at all possible that you have some underlying, limiting, unconscious beliefs around money that are stumbling your progress right now?

I think we both know the answer! So let's see if in the next section I have found some beliefs that you have that are screwing with your Wealth DNA.

19 Secrets Of The Wealthy

One of the things I find most compelling about the next section is that most of the differences between wealthy and struggling are in the mind; they are beliefs, driven by values. Every great wealth teacher has pointed that out in one way or another.

So it comes as no surprise that my own 19 secrets of the wealthy are mainly belief and mindset secrets. Make no mistake, though – the small differences in attitude and outlook will make all the difference in your results.

In case you have read or heard some of them before and already know them, great. Tick them off in your mind, nod in approval and be happy. Make sure, though, that you know what "knowing them already" actually means. Having heard them is one thing; living them and having manifested their conclusive result is another thing altogether. When all is said and done, there is always more said than done. Like another of my coaches once so poignantly remarked, "To know and not to do is not to know!"

If you already practice some or most of them, then look out for the one or two distinctions that will make the difference. If you are totally new to wealth mindset, just check in with yourself which ones resonate the most with you.

In simple terms you should be aware that if you are not as wealthy as you want to be, it's almost certainly a belief that deep down stops you from making it happen. You might not even know it's there and you might have been unconsciously carrying it for a long, long time, passed down from generations. There is no excuse to not being wealthy, especially if you live in the UK or the US or any other free market democracy!

So here they are – 19 beliefs that separate the wealthy from the struggling.

The Wealthy Create And Are Responsible.
The Poor Blame And Make Excuses.

Well I hope you read the chapter about crossing the line. It's pretty straightforward: If you live below the line and blame, complain and justify your results, then you are not taking charge. Living above the line, being responsible for your results and creating solutions for problems is what puts you in the driving seat.

One definition of business is "solving problems at a premium" – and if you create solutions for big problems, you can make big bucks. Smart entrepreneurs also aim to solve problems for more people (scale) with less of their time (leverage). Do the same.

Don't be at the mercy of someone giving you a handout. If I want to earn more, I can do something about it. I can create something and sell it.

The Wealthy Play To Win. The Poor Play Not To Lose.

Well, it might sound like a semantic difference – but this is profound. If you enter a game or race just not to lose, you're defending. If you are entering to win, you're attacking. You might think, What's the big deal? I still don't want to lose. Well, let me put it to you this way: Your chance of winning when you enter not to lose is practically zero. So success is all about increasing your odds of winning. And a winning attitude is one of them.

The Wealthy Commit To Wealth.
The Poor Dream About It Or Talk About It.

To decide and to commit are powerful acts that tell the world and the universe you are serious. To move aside and let you pass. Many studies have shown that when people are unclear or ambiguous about their goals they are a lot less likely to achieve them.

So when you talk about a wealth goal in a "maybe – let's see how it goes" kind of way, you'll be a lot less likely to achieve it. If you ever met a totally committed person – be it to his children, partner, health or wealth – you can feel the power. It's not the words that make it happen, it's the underlying drive to have to achieve it – no matter what. Move aside, obstacles!

The Wealthy Think Big. The Poor Think Small.

"If you aim for the stars, you'll hit the moon. If you aim for the fence, you hit the ground." I'm not sure where I heard that first, but it's clear to see that although you might not always get what you want and you may fall short of your expectations, if you aim higher and set big goals, you're a lot more likely to achieve them.

If you are working on your skill set and network, you can achieve more and more with less effort. It's all about what you perceive possible and what you can achieve. The next level of wealth is just outside your comfort zone. Re-read this. The next level of wealth is just outside what you are currently comfortable doing. You have what you have now because of what you do, and most people do what's within their comfort zone.

That's another reason why a higher-level peer group will be so conducive for your wealth. They'll make you think bigger and extend and stretch your comfort zone.

The Wealthy See Opportunity, The Poor See Problems

When I was broke, I remember looking around not seeing any opportunities at all. I was looking, but I wasn't seeing. My filters

160

weren't set to the right frequency. My skillset, mindset, contacts, knowledge – all of it was tuned into the problems and the reasons for the problems. Shit FM, I think was the frequency. There was only one listener on that frequency, because no one gives a shit about your problems.

Today my biggest problem is what to say no to. I get better and better opportunities offered to me. You become more, you get offered more. Success attracts success, money attracts money.

My guru used to say that a saint and a sinner walking down the road see a different world. So it is with a wealthy and a poor person. The wealthy see a wealth of opportunity, the poor see a lack of it.

The Wealthy Study Money. The Poor Think: "Money Is Against Them."

Now, this is one of the biggest things you must understand: Wealth is a study. Health is a study. Happiness is a study. You have to dedicate some time to study what you want to master. There are laws that govern everything in this universe. We don't understand them all and we don't need to. But we can spot the patterns and act according to the observed laws and rules.

There are laws to a relationship. There are laws to health. There are laws to spirituality. There are laws to wealth. So study wealth. Just as the wealthy do. You investing in yourself and reading this book shows me that you get the concept. Don't stop studying. Don't stop learning. Or as Steve Jobs in his commencement address of 2005 said: Stay hungry.

I came across the concept of everything being a study from Jim Rohn in his famous "How to Have Your Best Year Ever" seminar. Jim in this talk mentioned a book that has changed my life, The Richest Man in Babylon by George Clason.

I will recommend that book right now. I've recommend this book for many years and here's what I found. People who go out and buy this book and read the book become eventually financially free. But 97 per cent of people don't buy the book. Why would that be?

I bought the book. I've studied the laws of wealth. I bought hundreds of copies since and gave them to my students. It took some time. The knowledge had to be there first. Then it changed my feelings. Then I changed what I did. And guess what? The results just followed. This is what most people worry about the most, and actually that is the one thing you don't have to worry about at all. Results will follow if you study and apply what you learned.

I'm giving you the response-ability to go out and get the book. I told you already it'll be life-changing.

That is why events like Wealth Breakthrough Live are so great. Because you'll immerse yourself for three days in an environment, learning new skills and discovering new knowledge that is life-changing. And there is nothing like a live event. Nothing can match the power of an immersive experience like that.

The Wealthy Admire Other Wealthy People. Poor People Resent Them.

That was a big one for me: The wealthy admire other wealthy people. Let me tell you why is this so crucial. The way the human mind works is that it's hard to become what you despise. You will not manifest what you hate.

If I see a guy in a nice Bentley and think, Bastard! You must be a drug dealer. I hate you, and at the same time, I desire what he has, that will mess with my mind. It sends mixed signals. It's not a clear message to your subconscious. How can you put all systems go and switch to a higher gear going after what you want if you believe the person who has what you want is a hateful criminal? Unsurprisingly, your unconscious mind will keep you safely where you are – which is not wealthy.

I honestly admit that I found that quite hard. But I trained myself. I trained myself whenever I saw someone in the Bentley to say, "I admire you. Bless you. I would like to learn what you know about success and money."

So the next time you see someone in a Bentley, instead of thinking "drug dealer," why don't you tell them you love their car (don't say you'd love to have their car – it'll freak them out) and ask them what they do for business?

I promise you most of them are not drug dealers!

Now here is another one of my limiting beliefs I was able to eradicate. My friend Rob is really into his cars. I think he has six or seven or so, many of them really cool sports cars like Ferraris and Maseratis.

So he says to me, "Dan. You know what I love about driving my red Ferrari? People say I inspire them." No one was inspired when I had a F- reg Vauxhall Astra in "rust."

But I wasn't so sure about this one. I thought he was more after the envy and the admiration so I let it go.

As it played out he gave me his Ferrari to drive for my wedding in July. I pull into a petrol station on this sunny day in July. Roof down in the gleaming red Ferrari and I'm feeling at least an inch taller enjoying the looks and admiration of people around me. (Or were they just thinking "drug dealer"?)

At this point, a guy walks up to me and says, "Wow. I love your car. What do you do?" I told him that only a few years ago I delivered pizzas for Domino's and that I was broke back then and that I now ran my own business. He said, "Wow. This is really inspirational. Thank you."

Well, that was me learning another lesson. Don't judge what it'll be like to be wealthy and what effect it might have on other people. This short conversation most likely made his day! I drove away with tears in my eyes thinking, Maybe that will trigger him to change what he does; to change his Wealth DNA? Maybe he will say to his wife, "I met a guy today. He was a nice guy with a really cool car and a few years ago he was worse off than we are today. Now I believe we can have our dreams!"

So, you have to admire what you desire. You'll be amazed that people are happy to share and help you. Some wealthy people even run mastermind groups and pretty much let you buy a place at their table. That's a shortcut right there.

The Wealthy Have Wealthy Networks. The Poor Have Poor Ones.

You most likely have heard the phrase "your network is your net worth." Well – it's true. If I look at the property deal I've just done with Mark Homer as a JV partner, this is only possible because of the network I can tap into, which took me years to build. You don't build trust overnight. That's how the big-boys-networks work, of course.

So start pushing into higher-level networks and relationships. They are not always after money. Check what else you can bring to the table.

My first experience was back in 2005 when I helped a property multi- millionaire with his mentorship programme. I worked for free, offering my skills in audio and video recording to him. In exchange I was introduced into his network. Before I knew it, I was working alongside some of them doing business.

Here is an interesting slant on this age-old wisdom. John Demartini says, "Your self-worth is your net-worth." I think he's right there, as well. It actually comes first. If you don't value yourself, there is no way you can ever be part of a high- value and high-net worth network.

The Wealthy Know How To Market, Sell And Self-Promote, The Poor Don't.

Now, that doesn't just mean selling on a webinar or selling a course or being onstage or what generally constitutes selling. It also means to market and sell ideas. To excite people about your vision and to bring them on board and align them with your legacy. You're always selling something. If you have any discussion where you don't already agree on something, you have to sell it.

If two people enter a conversation, the one with the better belief in the argument and sales skills will win and influence and convince the other party. That how the world works. And wealthy people all know how to influence.

I'll give you an example. During one of our product launches we ran a webinar with "nothing for sale" – well, that was only partly true, because I did my level best to sell you into the idea of booking a consultation.

Poor people talk about selling as if it is something dirty. As a matter of fact nothing happens without a sale being made. The whole economy is based on transactions: exchanges of value using money.

So if you go out there and sell your product and service, you're always selling an idea first. I'm here to sell you an idea. And I hope that will lead to you and I working together for a long, long time. I'm doing my best to use the right stories, the right words, the right concepts – all of it to sell you the idea that Wealth DNA is your ticket to the life of your dreams.

There are your beliefs and there are mine, and I'll do what I can to sell you one of my core beliefs – that wealth is a learnable skill, a study.

Marketing has to be one of my favourite things in the world. I look at marketing as the skill of showing a product or service in its best light to help people make a decision to try it, to believe it will change their lives (or state). To get people to take any sort of action requires skill. Marketing, influence, sales, call it what you want – but wealthy people are not afraid to learn it and to use it, and they know that it is at the heart of any business.

The Wealthy Are Leaders, The Poor Are Followers.

I mentioned in my introduction that I was a follower for many years of my life. I accepted someone else's philosophy without proper introspection or diligence. I have since learned that it's best to be a student and then to become a leader, whilst still staying a humble student. Because the reality is that you either have your own plan or you're part of someone else's.

I wasn't just afraid of becoming a leader, I also wasn't clear about what skills a leader needs or where to learn them. Good news, leadership in its beginning pretty much means get up and move. Do anything with conviction and direction and you will attract a following and a student or fan base. If you move, you're on a mission. Define it well and communicate it well and you can get something going. Get people to believe in what you believe and you can get a tribe.

So if you have any legacy and purpose and you can get people to see a vision of it and let the world know about it, you'll be leading naturally.

Leadership is something you'll have to embrace. Wealthy people make decisions to serve their legacy and, if they have to, will make tough decisions for the longer term and greater good to protect it. That is leadership.

The Wealthy Know How To Leverage, The Poor Build Are Being Leveraged.

Remember the matrix of exchange of value? Well, it's pretty simple: the poor get leveraged by being employees working someone else's plan, doing the leg-work, doing what they can selling their time for money. That's the only model the poor know.

Instead the wealthy know how to leverage. There's only a few different things one can leverage. I use the mnemonic TIME, as in essence it's all about creating more time. As time is the most valuable commodity, how can you get more of it? You need to learn to leverage:

- Time
- Ideas
- Money
- Experience

Leveraging Time

You leverage time by using other people's time. Having them work for you. It's pretty obvious, really, but when I employed two outsourcers in the Philippines to work for me, I created more hours in the day, like the numbers shown earlier through Bill Gates. My 24 and another 48 from my outsourcers. Better than trying to squeeze 27 hours out of a day or having the stress of having that amount of work but never enough time. Plus you know what most people would do with their time if they had a few extra hours a day, don't you? That's right – fill it with the same shit they already filled it with! Amazing how you can work so long and not really achieve anything, isn't it? We've all been there. The wealthy simply outsource it all through virtual assistants, PAs, outsourcers, consultants and contractors and employees.

While we are out here in Dubai, I am with my business partner Rob Moore. He likes to take a few holidays a year to do strategic work, and he's just bought a new house literally the Friday before we left. He's doing it up: full refurb, home automation and all that. Now instead of getting his hands dirty and mucking in like most, he's had a dozen tradesmen – painters, wallpaper hangers, AV experts, floor fitters, carpet fitters, bespoke office designers, curtain makers – all giving his house a full top-to-bottom makeover, all while he's enjoying the dun and wealth in Dubai. Now that's leverage. His PA is project managing it, he keeps showing me all the photos of one job done and another job done and another job done, and when he gets home a removal company will move him in. That's leveraging people. It's also keeping a lot of people in work and moving money around his local economy. That's how the wealthy act and think.

Here is what John D. Rockefeller, one of the world's richest men, who used his fortune to fund ongoing philanthropic causes, said: "I would rather earn 1 per cent of a hundred people's efforts than 100 per cent of my own efforts." Thanks, John! Well, that's called leverage.

Now once you learn to manage those who you leverage (outsource to, employ) using systems, processes and managers, you'll get more time to do what leaders and the wealthy do: strategic planning and putting your money to work. And creating the lifestyle you desire.

You can also leverage time by using systems and software and all kinds of technology. For example I use an email system in my business and we're sending 500,000 to 1 million emails a month. Is that time leverage? You bet.

Leveraging Ideas

Smart wealthy people leverage other people's ideas. Why would you want to create every idea yourself? Books like this, courses and other valuable, proven information are all out there to shortcut your learning. Many poor people only adopt new ideas when they are forced to; the wealthy look to leverage other people's ideas and on the ground experience in their own business all the time.

Steve Jobs at Apple was famed for this. Although a company known for innovation, Apple frequently took existing technology and made it user friendly, simple and intuitive. Why reinvent the wheel? Someone has done all the heavy lifting so that you can get the easy ride. Leverage that. Don't be so creative and artistic thinking you need to innovate or create everything from scratch. You don't have to be the first to be original, because being original is putting your own spin and unique personality on things. There aren't that many new ideas left, so use the best existing ones.

You should use the ideas from this book. It's just smart leverage. Wealthy people don't want to learn and discover it all for themselves.

They use other people's ideas. Innovation is so overrated; it takes too long! It took me years to acquire the knowledge and experience that went into some of the ideas in this book. Use them

Another way to leverage people's ideas is to become part of a Mastermind. We run an Inner Circle Mastermind program (ICM) at Unlimited Success where a small group of successful or would-be successful business owners leverage each other's ideas in a roundtable, mastermind format. I'm facilitating and leading this Mastermind, but I also sit in on a different Mastermind group where I am one of the peer/students; as I see this as a valuable way to accelerate my results and learning.

Leveraging Money

This is of course why property is so powerful. Banks lend you a huge portion of the asset value, and you leverage all of the uplift. So, you're leveraging your money. Let's say you put down a 10 per cent deposit and the market goes up by 10 per cent; you have in essence made a 100 per cent return on your investment (I left out finance costs for ease of calculation).

You might be already using this in your wealth creation, or you might be thinking about this for the first time. But the wealthy have been leveraging money since the beginning of money.

That's what banks are doing. Giving you a couple of per cent interest, while they lend it out to make more money on your money.

Compound interest – it's magic, right? Leveraging money. Borrowing money from other people. Using money to make money and reinvesting it to make more money on the money that made you money. And so it snowballs. Just remember compounding works in reverse, too, so get rid of that bad debt and start compounding leveraged money the right way.

Leveraging Experience

Leveraging people's experience is bringing their experience into your business. Every time you hire a coach or mentor or have a member of your team help you achieve your goals, you leverage their experience. They've spent years gaining all the experience, blazing the trail, sweating all the sweat, and you come in and get your results through them. This is not just a guaranteed shortcut to success; it also protects you from potentially costly mistakes.

Many people don't call on others for experience because they are worried about looking stupid, being powerless or humbled or having to take orders from others. Others want to scrimp and save the extra money, thinking they can do it themselves. They save a little money, but it costs them more, and there is an opportunity cost of that time, which ended up costing more. You won't find these traits that often in the wealthy.

When you employ experts in their field as you expand your business, you are leveraging their experience. Very simply, you pay them according to their experience and the value they bring to your business. Richard Branson said that the biggest secret to success was to hire the best people he could get his hands on.

The Wealthy Keep Going And Add To Their Assets, The Poor Keep Starting Again And Again And Again

Keep it going when the going gets tough. Keep on keeping on and the main thing is to keep the main thing the main thing. We all want results fast, sure, but the wealthy understand the lag time and long-term planning and strategy. That is why it is important to have a legacy through purpose and have your own life plan, so you know where you are going and, more importantly, why you are going there. It will also keep you going when you have hard days, which you will. This book isn't about meditating away the hard times and being positive all the time when underneath you want to flip out; it is about having a higher legacy and purpose so you make your hard days as good as hard days can be and you see the lessons in them that you need to get to create more wealth.

How do wealthy people make a decision on what to take on and what to say no to? If it ain't serving the higher purpose it won't become part of the plan. Learn to say no to distracting opportunities and keep doing what you're doing.

I've found that hard in the past. I spent so many years not having any opportunities that when they started coming along I wanted to say yes to all of them. Hey, I'm an entrepreneur; that's what we do. Plus I don't want to miss out on anything. But in the end, starting again resets you to zero, and you have to go through all the hard graft at the start again, just in a different niche. Plus you can find yourself running away from hard things, thinking that the grass will be greener on the other side, and of course it never is. If it takes 80 per cent of the fuel of a rocket just to get it off the ground, then it's dumb to burn all that fuel, just get off the ground, then park the rocket and start up the next one. But that's what poor people keep doing, and they get no momentum, compounding or longevity. They don't become known for anything.

Poor people change all the time: new ventures, new ideas, new excitement. It's going to be different this time, Rodney. Great at starting, poor at finishing. The wealthy know that pretty much all of the money is made towards the end of the journey. Just like compounding, where all the real gains are at the end.

Poor people leave the field before the harvest time. They don't understand the timing of the universe and the seasons.

Unlike a job, a business has the advantage of momentum and automation. For example, my Amazon business was a bit of work to set up, but I haven't touched it for months now, and it's making me money every day – even in my sleep! Though I must admit it takes 15 seconds to log in and look at the sales in the last hour, and it does take a few seconds to keep hitting the refresh button.

But you have to stay the course. Wealthy people do. Just a word of warning though: make sure you stick with business models that have a high chance of succeeding. Or it's just called being stubborn!

The Wealthy Give, The Poor Take.

In most people's minds it's the greedy rich that exploit the poor. Well think again. Warren Buffet and Bill Gates have launched the $600 billion challenge, asking billionaires to give away half of their wealth. Buffet and Gates have personally given away tens of billions of dollars to charities and causes of their choice.

In 2013 alone the "Philanthropic 50" gave $7.7 billion to charity. In 2006 Warren Buffet gave $43 billion to charity. Check out philanthropy. com to be impressed and change your view of the wealthy. Let go of the nonsense you might believe about the wealthy, because the wealthiest in the world have proven to be the most giving.

So – I'm not knocking or belittling the common people's efforts to help. For example, the BBC has since 1980 raised £600 million for children in need. That is the whole of the UK over 35 years! It's pretty staggering, but Facebook's Mark Zuckerberg has given almost $1 billion in 2014 on his own. That puts it into perspective, right?

And it's the poor who are taking, from free healthcare to subsidies to benefits. The poor drain the financial resources of the government if they are not working, paying taxes and contributing to society and doing their bit for their community. I'm not taking pot shots at the poor; some people are genuinely less fortunate, but there are many people who just have a bad Wealth DNA. And you know how that can change. You are reading this book and you know a better way.

The Wealthy Master Money, The Poor Are Slaves To Money.

They way I see it there are really three layers to mastering money. And the rich and wealthy do all three of them radically differently to the poor and struggling.

Here are the three parts of money mastery:

- *Learn to attract and make it*
- *Learn to keep and manage it*
- *Learn to invest and grow it.*

These are three separate sets of skills. Is it possible that someone can be good at making it yet have nothing to show for it? Could someone earn a lot but spend even more? Is it possible that someone is excellent at managing very little money? Of course it is. But even both these skills will not lead you to wealth and fulfilment. It's obvious you need to learn and master all three, and Wealth DNA is theguidebook to understand the proven principles to lasting wealth through the 4 Cs, especially the first C, cashflow.

By the way, if you have learned to attract and make it but it seems to slip through your fingers, you might have an underlying sabotaging money belief. I did for 20 years. I didn't think I deserved money, so if any came my way, I would just give it away thoughtlessly to get rid of the guilt and shame. Of course it was all subconscious.

Or you just need to learn to manage it!

The Wealthy Have Money Work Hard For Them. The Poor Work Hard For Their Money.

By now we all know that our goal it to reduce our dependence on earned Income and have our desired lifestyle paid by leveraged income from Assets. So when the wealthy make more money from their money, then that is exactly what that means. Investors measure the attractiveness of an investment by its 'cash on cash return'. What money do I get out for the amount of money I put in and how fast and securely?

Have your money work hard for you! If you could invest some of your business profits into a property deal, where you get all the money out within the year, plus create £500k in equity and £3,000 in net cashflow a month, and have multiple other ways to monetize the remaining land on the property, would you class that as a good investment? I did. That's why I went for it.

That's what I learned when I changed my Wealth DNA. To think and act like the wealthy do; to follow the rules and strategies in Wealth DNA.

If I remind myself of the days as a pizza delivery guy for Dominos, well that was 'working hard for my money'!

The Wealthy Learn And Grow.
The Poor Think They Already Know.

I start this secret or belief with a story about my friend and business partner Rob Moore. I have known Rob since 2007 and in January 2008 he attended one of my courses. He was already quite successful back then and definitely the most experienced businessman and marketer in the room.

But guess who took more notes than anybody else? Rob. Every time we meet, Rob takes more notes than anybody else. Every time we meet, Rob studies and learns new stuff. This year alone he will have listened to 100 new audio books!

So in ten years, he will have consumed the content of 1,000 books. Wow. You fall over wealth when you act like that, you can't not attract it.

I'm no stranger to lifelong learning, myself. This year I will have spent about $50,000 in educating myself to learn from the best. I went to the best in the US to build my Amazon business, investing in expensive but valuable courses and of course all the travel and hotels and time away from my existing businesses.

But I've already made twice that investment back, and we're right at the start of the trend curve. I always want to be ahead and to know about upcoming trends and how to react to them or utilise them for profit and leverage.

When I go anywhere, jump on any course or training, I'm always looking to gain some insights and never want to be the smartest guy in the room. I only need one key distinction and I know I will get a return. If you just remember one key element of this book, you will get a return on your investment.

But in contrast many poor and struggling people have an air of arrogance and know it all attitude about them, which will lock them firmly in the poverty zone. It's their mindset that stops them from acquiring the skillset that will keep them upset! Or they're scared of looking silly. Or it's just never occurred to them.

The Wealthy Have Healthy Skepticism.
The Poor Have Unhealthy Skepticism.

Skepticism is important, to a point. But there is a moment when the due diligence is done. When you have to trust your gut and focus on what you will do to make it work. Focus is such a powerful force, and you can't focus forward if you are overly skeptical of everything.

If it sounds good, you have to be skeptical to the point of doing research, de-risking and getting some proof, but you cannot let the skepticism control you or stop you. You can probably only plan, prepare or do research on 80 per cent of the leg work; then you have to make a decision, and fast. If the data says (80 per cent) yes, say yes! Decide now, and the rest of the 20 per cent you will learn along the way with your abilities and your resourcefulness.

The Wealthy Manage Their Fear.
The Poor Are Managed By Fear.

Let me tell you right now that fear will not disappear. Fear is part of life. To fear is to be human, and fear is a valuable auto-response in certain life situations. It's just that we don't handle it very well in non-threatening life scenarios. The wealthy have developed courage de-risking strategies and have all worked on ways to manage their fear. The only fear you should fear is fear itself.

I have personally struggled with this for most of my life and have because of this done many workshops and courses on fear and how to manage it. So here is what I learned about fear.

One of the main ways to deal with fear is to expose yourself to it in a controlled environment. Start small, so you don't get consumed by fear or fail too big and too fast. But you've got to do it, right away. Just like an inoculating injection is actually a little bit of the virus, you've got to experience the exact fear full on to beat it. There is no other way around it, but people spend their whole lives trying to find it.

Ralph Waldo Emerson said, "Do the thing you fear, and the death of fear is certain." That is true in many cases, as once you have faced your fear and found the fear unfounded, how can you fear it again? You've seen the proof and the reality and you realised all the fear was in your head.

Our unconscious mind creates all kinds of negative scenarios in an attempt to protect us, but remember that its job is to protect you and keep you safe, not to help you reach wealth and fulfilment. Our fears have not evolved as fast as the world we live in, so we fear small things like public speaking and asking someone out on a date as much as we do severe heights or death (which we really should fear).

I've walked multiple times over glowing coals, have broken arrows with my throat and done all kinds of things to build references in my memory that I can do things that my mind doesn't believe I can. And man, you feel great when you beat it. But all you are beating is the imagined reality in your head that never happens that way anyway!

One of the best definitions I ever heard is based on the astonishing fact that fear and excitement are biochemically the same. So how come we love one and want to avoid the other?

It appears that with excitement we anticipate a pleasurable outcome, while with fear we anticipate future pain. So nothing actually has yet happened, but it's the anticipation that creates the emotion.

Wealthy and successful people have learned to manage this self-talk, helped by references of past success or their peers and mentors. They have learned a better response mechanism, to feel the fear and to go for it. They know you can't hide from it because it will sabotage your wealth. They know what is on the other side of fear (everything they want), and that they have two easy choices: don't do it and forever regret it, keep telling yourself stories as to why you never did it ... or do it and collect the money, honey.

A Word On Wealth Distribution

One of the most common beliefs around money is that it isn't fairly distributed. Again and again politicians propose some utopian plan about fairer redistribution. And you might even subscribe to the notion of fair distribution. But what all of these proposed solutions don't take into consideration is that money has its own laws and rules.

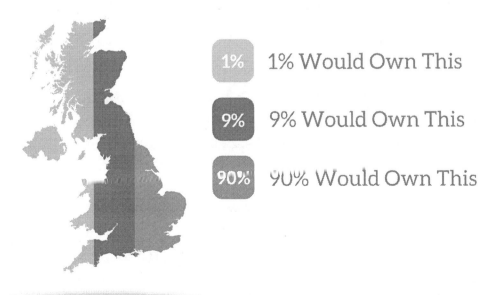

1% — 1% Would Own This

9% — 9% Would Own This

90% — 90% Would Own This

As a matter of fact, even if you had the power to distribute all the money in the world evenly so that every single human being had the same amount, what would happen?

Within just days the redistribution would begin and within a few weeks or months it would find its way back to all the people who know how to attract, manage and grow money. Their knowledge of the 4 Cs, their skills in trading, communicating, marketing and selling, offering solutions and helping people will make them money magnets.

So looking at the map again, it's clear that 1 per cent own about a third of the wealth, with another 9 per cent owning the second third, and the other 90 per cent having to share the remaining third. To spell it out more clearly, if you want to be in the top 10 per cent of earners in the UK for a couple, you only have to earn more than £151,400 a year (numbers based on treasury figures from March 2014)! That's surprisingly low (and easy), isn't it?

In the UK, the richest 1 per cent pull in about 14 per cent of all income. There are currently 73 billionaires in the UK, up from 53 the previous year, according to the latest Sunday Times Rich List. It's getting easier and more common.

The Forbes list of the world's richest people lists more than 1,200 billionaires across the globe, with Russia and China boasting more than 100 billionaires each. The US has more than 400 billionaires, and Microsoft founder Bill Gates is top with a net worth of $59 billion.

Simply put, over the last quarter century (1979 to 2007 to be exact), the top 1 per cent of income earners enjoyed far, far bigger real income gains than the other 99 per cent. Or simply put – the rich really do get richer (CBO report).

But before you go protesting in the streets, just know this: The richest 1 per cent of Americans pay 24 per cent of federal taxes! So the rich also contribute the most to the state and the economy by paying their taxes. It's not more than they have to, but almost a quarter of all contributions! But you know that now, because you know how money works: You know that currency is flow and the wealthy create more flow. You know that the rich give the most away, create most of the jobs and fuel the greater part of the economy.

These are the facts. And here is what some people choose to do: join the Occupy Movement and protest against the status quo. Here is what I suggest you do: Find out what you can do to move from the 90 per cent of people to the 9 per cent or from the 9 per cent to the 1 per cent. When you get there, become a philanthropist if giving is important to you. But you can't give what you haven't got, and the best way to make a difference is to make yourself wealthy, not campaign to take it off everyone else.

It's not just that the top 1 per cent have different toys and assets; their minds are different. They have created different neural pathways, habits and therefore results. How they think about money and wealth, how they feel about money and wealth, how they act about money and wealth is different from the majority.

The advice to "observe the masses and do the opposite" has been attributed to many people, including Walt Disney – but the lasting wisdom is this: If you don't want what the majority has, you have to do what the majority of people don't do or aren't prepared to do.

And that means – live above the line, take response-ability for your actions and results, and change your Wealth DNA!

Living in the UK is literally living in a land of opportunity. There are few countries in the world I know that are more supportive of entrepreneurs. I'm not just saying that; I was born in Austria, have travelled around the world and genuinely found this to be true. Compared to many countries there is quite little red tape, and there is all the infrastructure you need and the political and religious liberalism to pretty much do what you want! Certainly this is true when it comes to setting up a business, creating enterprise and jobs, making money and then benefitting from tax shelters.

If you keep doing what you're doing, you'll be getting what you're getting - or worse. With the world becoming more competitive, what got you a good enough result last year might not be good enough in the years to come. If you're not growing, you're dying. Keeping up is getting ahead, not staying the same.

And as you're out of school, you have to get yourself back into education. Work on yourself. Change your DNA. Change your thinking; the results will follow – guaranteed.

You might be reading this and have doubts or are being skeptical. And that's OK. It makes sense. If you don't have experiences that can serve as references for these new beliefs, then of course you are doubtful. You don't know what you don't know. But there is one thing that dispels all doubt, and that's proof. Create proof and see your self-doubt wane. But the creating proof has to start with you. You can't wait for the proof before you start. That's like saying to the wood burning stove, "Give me some heat and then I'll give you some wood and light it."

Let's come back to the distribution of wealth and how you can get a bigger share of it. The questions are simple:

182

"What do the people in the 1% do differently?"

"Is it possible to become one of them?"

"What is it that they do?"

"What is it they read?"

"What is it that they believe?"

"Who is it that they hang out with?"

"Which vehicles of Wealth did they choose?"

How many of those people do you think rely on a job?

I just want to make sure that you are aware and remind yourself that we're living in one of the most privileged countries in the world. We are sitting in a place where you can truly create wealth if you wanted to. London is still one of the financial capitals of the world. It's all around you when you know where to look. You can't use the outside world as an excuse in the privileged developed world we live in and the empire that is the UK.

If you're hoping, by the way, that money will solve all your problems, think again. The purpose of life is not to get rid of all problems. The purpose of life is to solve more problems with ease because you have the resourcefulness and skills and response-ability. And you can actually contribute to society and help the world whilst solving those problems. So embrace them and become someone who is good at solving them for others, and wealth will flow your way.

The Invisible Competitor

The biggest barrier to your success is you. The biggest competitor to yourself is you. The easiest person to lie to is you. The invisible competitor to you, is - you guessed it - you. This can be the noose around your neck that gains weight over time, or it can be used in the most highly honed and powerful way to achieve your legacy through purpose.

Your competition is imagined, your FEAR is imagined (False Evidence Appearing Real) and your limitations are imagined. They are projected realities of how (good or bad) something will happen, before it has even happened. And because you can't predict the future, you have no basis for the facts you are imagining anyway, and they are only serving to disempower you.

Have you ever had an argument with someone ... in your head?

Yes that's right. Have you ever played out an argument in your mind with full-scale anger but all in your own imagination? Have you ever received an email and read it a certain way and spent the rest of the day replaying it in your mind? Crazy, right? Totally insane to play in your mind a movie about something that hasn't happened yet, that has virtually zero chance of being like that in reality. Yet that is how most people spend most of their waking lives; thinking they know how someone will react or how a given situation will be, mostly in the negative, before it has even happened.

This is fear. This is doubt. This is shame and envy and guilt. These are all past or future scenarios that are not reality. But if unchecked they will become your disempowering reality.

But the same can be done in the positive, by visualisation. A positive, empowering reality can be manifested by changing what we predict in our minds a given situation will be. How many athletes vision smacking into the hurdle and falling on their face before they run their race? How many golfers envision doffing it straight into the bunker? Creating the vision of course is no guarantee for it to happen they way you want it, but it'll increase the odds.

So take control of the invisible competitor that is you. If you are going to imagine a reality, imagine a positive reality. If you are going to think, you might as well think big. If you are going to compete with anyone, don't compete with others, better your own best. Compete positively with yourself. Use last year as your yardstick for this year and next year as your target, and don't compare yourself to others who are on a different path.

And note down all your goals in Evernote or any app that you can use across all devices. That way you can track back each year and self fulfil your success progress compared to the years gone by. It's very inspiring. I remember being at Rob's house when we first conceived Wealth DNA, and we dug out a load of my early course notes on money. I pulled out a diary I used to keep and notes I'd made from a wealth training, and I set a goal back then in 2005 to make $1 online. I'm not joking. I got quite tearful; there was a time when making $1 online was a challenging goal. Looking back at it now, pulling in many millions, it is humbling and self-inspiring. And reading it here is having the same effect.

Becoming A Higher Level Person
Become a higher-level person and you solve higher-level problems. As I already mentioned before, the purpose of life is not to have zero problems. The purpose of life is to solve more problems with ease because you have the resourcefulness and skills and response-ability.

And you can actually contribute to society and help the world. You become a higher-level problem solver.

So when you have more money you will have different problems. It's not that money is the answer to the current problems; it is that your problems will scale up as the money scales up. Your job is to solve what I call higher-level problems. The previous level becomes normal/easy, and you grow into the next level.

Let's create - for this discussion - an arbitrary scale from 1-10. Level 1 means (easy peasy lemon squeezy) easy and level 10 means (no fricking way I'll minimum die) hard and complex.

If you were a level 1 person in terms of skill, resourcefulness, network and ability, what kind or problems could you solve? Well, the answer is pretty obvious. Only a level 1 problem. Even a level 2 problem would be way beyond your ability and seem like it could end the world as we know it.

Before I expand on this, let me be clear that this is no judgment on you or anyone as a human being or your value in society or your local community or family or church – but it is a reality of the world of wealth and money that people who solve the big complex problems get paid the big bucks.

You didn't buy this book for me to be warm and fluffy and cuddly (though I am in real life) and lie to you. You bought this book because you wanted to change something about your current wealth results; and that takes honesty from both of us. You made a commitment; you bought, you read and you are here. My commitment to you is honesty. To change your Wealth DNA, all you have to focus on is how you can solve bigger problems.

Once you have grown to be a level 2 person (whatever that means), you can indeed solve a level 2 problem. Only just and it will take all your effort and focus. But now a level 1 problem is easy and normal and no longer a problem.

So what if you worked hard on yourself, changed your peer group, learned new skills, worked on your wealth mindset over the next 12 months, were part of a higher level mastermind and more? Could you become a level 4 person? Of course you could. So what would that mean if you then had to tackle a level 2 problem? You'd hardly even register is as a problem. It'd be totally inside your comfort zone. It'd be easy. Done. Move on. Next.

Try to imagine (which is hard as you have no reference and personal experience for it yet in your life) being a level 10 person.

For example, if you wanted to join the B-Team (check it out at bteam. org) you'd have to be a level 10 – minimum. You'd be hanging out with Richard Branson and Jochen Zeitz (former CEO of Puma and now 100 per cent dedicated to sustainable development). Possible? Of course.

One definition of doing business is "solving problems for a premium." So if you want to make more money, all you have to do is solve bigger problems for more people. If you then add one more criteria to this simple equation of wealth, solve higher-level problems with less of your time by using all the tools of leverage we discuss in this book: people, systems, technology, ideas, money. Then your Wealth DNA will be radically different. You will create your own high-level code.

Personal Growth
Personal growth is all about becoming the person you want to be and subscribing to the notion of constant and never ending improvement.

It is about becoming the person you need to be to fulfil your legacy. It is about embracing all events that take you to that goal, many of them wrapped and disguised In challenge or difficulty. It is about seeing the good in every bad and the bad in every good. It is about becoming graceful under pressure, like a diamond that is carbon like everything else but came to shine and sparkle under intense pressure in the right environment.

Growth, according to Tony Robbins, is one of the six human needs, and one of the two that actually creates fulfilment, the second one being "contribution beyond yourself." Without growth there is no hope, and without hope there is no will to survive or better your situation.

In order to grow, you need to become someone more. In order to become someone more, you need to learn and gain experience.

From my experience the best way to accelerate your learning to become a higher-level person and to keep growing is to consume information and experience through books, audiobooks, courses and workshops, mentors, accountability and support groups and masterminds.

Let's look at this with a bit of Dan-style research (OK, I got my outsourcer to do most of this for me). I believe that it's actually quite easy to become a higher-level problem solver, because most people are not actively pursuing self-improvement and personal growth.

The shocking statistics are: 1/3 of households in the UK don't have a single book in them. 57 per cent of books read are not finished. 42 per cent of college students never read a book again after leaving college.

One of my mentors used to say, "Those that don't read have no advantage over those that can't read." We all know thanks to books and the Internet that information is free, shared and virtually limitless; all this success and "how-to" at our fingertips, yet most people don't take it and use it.

If you were to just read 15 minutes a day, you would read one million words in a year. Warren Buffett had read every book in his state library on business and investing by the age of 12. My (admittedly fairly intense) friend Rob Moore has listened to 100 audiobooks this year alone (as he listens to his audio on 2x speed)!

Sounds corny, but the more you learn, the more you earn. If you want to become great, study how to become great in your chosen field. Consume the knowledge and become the best habitually and unconsciously. And I wouldn't want to leave you without this little cheesy nugget: "Leaders are readers!"

With technological progress, it is even easier than ever before. Even fewer excuses. Before you had to trawl through books; now you can use a search bar in Amazon or Google or Facebook and have every niche at your fingertips, organised and distilled and presented in a palatable and actionable fashion by someone who is a genuine expert in the field, all for less than a tenner delivered to your door. E-book readers can store hundreds of books; Audible and iTunes allow you to store and listen to dozens of audio books on your smart phones and all for the price of a couple of cups of coffee. The democratization of wealth is closely linked the democratization of information.

And if that is too much effort for you, you can hire an outsourcer or virtual assistant to research the niche topics for you (like I did for some of this book), find the audio versions for you, download them onto your mobile device, buy you headphones (on Amazon) and you can plug and play!

Even if you're busy, you can consume the information while walking, in the gym or car or plane, or even on the toilet (OK – that's maybe a bit much!). No time is dead time anymore. I can't advise strongly enough to get into the habit of reading/listening and studying. Use audio to do it on otherwise dead time, and you could consume 50 books a year with no more effort. That is millions of words that are automatically programming your brain for success and wealth.

I think audio books are great, but I do both. Read and listen. Somehow the knowledge goes deeper. We created an audio book of Wealth DNA, as well, so you can get the knowledge in two ways! If you get the audio version, too, then you can programme your subconscious mind to pull wealth into your life. Listen before you go to bed and when you wake up for maximum programming effect.

To take it to the next level of memory, retention and advancement of information, I have for years now invested a good portion of my income into courses, workshops and trainings, not just books. I call myself a bona fide "course junkie," always the first one to run to the back of the room and sign up for every course! That's how I learned about internet marketing, sales, public speaking, NLP, direct response marketing, e-commerce, personal development, wealth and money making, Forex, spread betting, property and much more.

Most people would think nothing of the conventional wisdom of going to university to study something they probably will never use (according to Forbes, it is 60 per cent) and spend over £55,000 on fees, student loans and rent. Now, of course, university serves a purpose, but more so for the government to get people into the tax paying system or for specialist services than for entrepreneurs to make a living through legacy.

With that same £55,000 you could invest in just about every course in the specific chosen fields you need to master, go directly to the experts, even get one to one mentoring and accountability programmes with them. You could be in their Inner Circle being held accountable and regularly coached to overcome the challenges that are now easy to them. You could travel the world with them, get shortcut introductions to their high-level network and have instant seven-, eight- and nine-figure connections in every field, and you could buy a Porsche with the change.

Network

Nothing is more important than your human connections. Many times we call it the network. Think about it. Have you heard about the theory of six degrees of separation? It proposes that anyone on the planet can be connected to any other person on the planet through a chain of acquaintances that has no more than five additional intermediaries. The theory was first proposed in 1929 by the Hungarian writer Frigyes Karinthy in a short story called "Chains."

It has been proven many times since and in today's world of social media it's most probable that you are connected to almost anyone one the planet by just two or three degrees of separation.

Interestingly a site called Six Degrees, launched in 1997, is considered to be the first social networking site and the precursor of sites like Facebook, Twitter and LinkedIn, which have effectively lowered the number of intermediaries in the chain, arguably to almost zero.

If you're active on LinkedIn you can see how big your network is if you look at how many people you are connected to via your first-level connections. You can have an online friends list and see friends of friends. Someone probably knew someone who you know and added you as a friend, and they are from Australia!

Most likely the money you need for your venture, the deal you are looking for, the business partner you're missing, the perfect client you are searching for is indeed very close and either inside or just outside your current network, connected to you via one or two degrees of separation.

Your Net Worth – The Shocking Truth

You might have heard the theory that your income is pretty much the average of the five (or in other explanations, ten) people you spend most of your time with.

You can either just believe me or put this theory to the test by writing down the five people who you spend most time with on a daily basis and check if your lifestyle and income is radically different. Chances are they aren't. The same will be true for your net worth.

In fact, why don't you do it now. Go on, write down the top 5-10 people you spend most of your time with...

Now that you have done it, look at that list and ask yourself:

"How many are millionaires or billionaires?"

"How many run huge enterprises?"

"How many are philanthropists?"

"How many are one of the best at the thing they do in the world?"

"And how many are 'losers'?"

OK, don't answer that last question, but you get where I'm coming from. You are looking at a list that represents your network and also - who you are; like looking into a mirror that exaggerates your strengths and weaknesses.

This is why on your journey to change your Wealth DNA you will most likely lose some of your current peer group. The reason is simple: different groups hold themselves to different standards. If your standards change your peer group will change. Don't fear this, don't let this hold you back – it's a natural process. Don't let them drag you back; don't feel that you owe them anything. Just be clear on your path and be grateful for the people you meet along the way and the people you wave goodbye to.

Tony Robbins is quoted of having said that 'the quality of your life is a direct reflection of the expectations of your peer group'. Read this sentence again. It's profound.

Think about it and make sure you understand what it means. It's the level of expectations from you of the people around you that is the most determining factor of success. It is the standards they hold you to. If you have a peer group with low standards or low expectations, they will continuously try to pull you down or keep you there. Not because they don't love you, but because they DO love you but don't want to lose that connection. You reaching out of the group and holding yourself to a higher standard makes them feel scared and insecure.

When I look back at my life, many of my old friends and relatives (who are still trapped in the rat race) told me, "Don't work so much. Give yourself a break." And when I meet them today, there is not that much we share, there is very little to talk about. And that's OK.

I'm glad I moved on and I love my new peer group.

What Robbins suggests, as well, is that you make sure that in every area of your life, personal and professional, there is a core group of people with higher standards and expectations than your own. They will lift you up, inspire you, stimulate you, challenge you and ensure you will reach your goals.

Think about this: If you are a tennis player and you want to improve, who do you play with? Opponents that are weaker or stronger than you? From whom do you learn the most? You know the answer, but you know how it makes you feel in the presence of those better than you. It is those feelings you need to manage and grow away from. Remember what they are great at, you can learn from. And you are great at something they could learn from you. No one is better or worse than anyone else; we all have our own set of gifts and learned talents that we get to share with others.

So the key question is:

"Have you consciously chosen your current peer group?"

And another key question is:

"Do you have the opportunity to join a higher level peer group?"

I have run Mastermind Programs and Inner Circle Business Coaching groups for many years now. You literally buy yourself another peer group. My advice? Get into the highest level you get access to, even if you think you can't afford it. Ask yourself instead, Can you afford not to do it?

Some of these groups have strict criteria; often a good attitude and being able to cough up the entrance fee is enough. Before I carry on and tell you the three different groups you must cultivate your network with, let me clear up a huge misconception:

"Peer pressure is bad!"

Peer Pressure Vs Peer Power

Peer pressure is commonly associated with something negative: the loss of individuality and identity to fit into a group. Well, let me make a distinction here about how the pressure from your peer group can actually be the most stimulating experience for your personal growth and purpose and the most important ingredient to change your Wealth DNA. I call this variation "peer power." So what determines the difference between the negative peer pressure and the positive peer power? Well, just answer this simple question:

"Does the pressure you experience in your peer group make you into a smaller and less expressive person pushing you to give up on your hopes and ideals?"

Or...

"Does the pressure around you make you push harder to excel, achieve more and expand your comfort zone and have bigger dreams?"

"Are the people in your peer group supportive and helping you towards your goals?"

Well the latter questions would be peer power, and it's the most obvious and most overlooked secret to change your Wealth DNA.

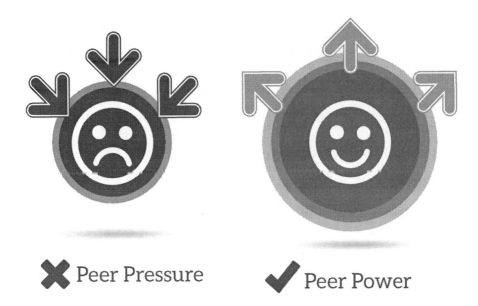

❌ Peer Pressure   ✔️ Peer Power

The people you hang out with are the most important part of your success. Full stop. Why? Because they will hold you to a different and higher standard. If you hang out with millionaires and multi-millionaires, what kind of standards will they have for their life? In terms of performance, work ethic, self respect, health, self-development, growth?

If all your mates go to Cayman for four weeks in February and you can only afford a weekend in Blackpool, how long would they be your mates? Not very long! Not very long because there are only two things you can do: either you shape up and you get to their level or you get out because you can't stand the pressure. Actually, it's not so much the pressure – it's the embarrassment. It's the shame that'll make you get out of that peer group. It's that mirror right in front of your face just a bit too close for comfort. And when you leave you'll have a bunch of excuses to justify it. I know – because that's what I did before I finally decided to shape up and change my Wealth DNA.

Change your peer group, change your life.

The Three Different Networks You Must Cultivate

From my experience there are three distinct and different parts of your network you should cultivate (only if you want to be wealthy). They are separate, because they require different strategies, communication messages and have different objectives.

Here they are:

Followers and Audience
Peers and Colleagues
Gurus and Teachers
Followers and Audience

Keep building the database. One of the assets I have continually built since 2006 is my database: my list of students, prospects, customers. Ideally you hold them in a software designed to hold data, communicate with them in an intelligent way (automated, personalised and segmented) and receive money for selling the products and services, as well.

Your audience is the amount of people that are listening to you (from the Latin word audio, to listen). If your audience is small and not attentive, you'll have a hard time exchanging value, which means making money.

The second part of this is of course to widen your reach via social media: Facebook, LinkedIn, Twitter, Google+, Pinterest and Instagram. You don't have to be on all of them, or you could be on more of them, but you can't ignore the opportunity to connect with potentially billluns of people at pretty much no cost. Choose your weapon!

To avoid the time suck, either dedicate a fixed amount of time every day or week or outsource your social media to your outsourcer, VA or PA.

My dad worked for the Austrian equivalent of the BBC. In his day, if you wanted to reach a big audience, you only had two choices: national press or radio and TV. Both of them required you to have deep pockets! Not for "normal" people. The world is very different now, right?

In one of my talks I share the little nugget that "the bigger your audience, the bigger the paycheck." Well, there is a little bit more to it, but in essence it's true. If you have millions of people who want to know what you have to say and teach, you can make millions of pounds..

Peers And Colleagues

What I call peers and colleagues would have been called competition in the old days. Today I've trained myself to have an abundance mindset and talk about co-opetition. Working separately but together to help each other. It's collaboration with your competition. And one of the reasons is that through technology we all have international or national businesses. You don't own an area anymore, so you have to learn to share in a mutually profitable way.

I've focused on cultivating these peer relationships with people in my industry, and it paid off big time. The reason why this makes sense is because you will have customers on your database that have bought all you have to sell and are still looking for other solutions. Or they might not need or want what you have to offer. So by partnering and doing a JV, everybody wins, and you are leveraging the trust your JV partner has built over years with his or her subscriber base, their audience.

There are many smart and simple profit-sharing models around.

All I would say is this: Join or create a peer group of like-minded people in your industry or people you want to do business with. You can join the Wealth DNA community on Facebook. I'll be there, and depending on the stage of this book launch and its success, so will many other like-minded peers.

Gurus And Teachers

This is easy. Find the people that are gurus (or even bigger gurus than you!) in your industry. There is always another level. And if you can, join their network or group. In 2014 alone I've spent about $50,000 to be in the presence of the next-level entrepreneurs I wanted to learn from. Please note I use the word guru in a positive light and its original meaning of teacher. I'm talking about knowledgeable people, leaders and teachers you can learn from.

The cool thing is that a handful of them (the ones I strategically targeted) have now become peers, and we're making a lot of money together. I've become a higher-level person by hanging out with higher-level people. Amazing, right? Don't be afraid to ask, don't be afraid to work your ass off to show them you're good. And remember, you have unique skills, learned talents and experiences to bring to the table.

Summary

Who you are and what's most important to you drives what level of wealth you will create in your life, in all areas of your life. Your Wealth DNA is hidden in your values. If you want more money, move wealth or money up your values list and start to live according to the new order. It's not what happens to you, it's how you deal with what happens to you that counts; do you react like a leader with purpose or a victim with excuses?

Your beliefs drive your thoughts, your thoughts become feelings and feelings become things. Take control of what you believe and how you play out a result in your mind, and your results will change accordingly. Learn the best from the rich and successful and drop the rest; change your network to change your net worth.

You can control your third C, character, and intentionally take full ownership of who you want to become. And your wealth will continually compound and grow because you will continually grow. Who do you need to become to be, do and have more wealth in your life?

One of my favourite Jim Rohn quotes is, "Become a millionaire. Not for the money, but for the person you have to become to achieve it!" Well said, Mr Rohn.

The Wealth Diamond:
The 4th C - Communication

The fourth C in the Wealth Diamond is communication. Communication is your message, the way it is delivered to the world and the route for your customers, clients and network to reach you. The fourth C completes the Wealth Diamond.

Communication is two-way: the way you find the world and the way the world finds you. Without this C, the other 3 Cs have no outlet.

Communication is how you share your message and how you are known by the world. It is your values as seen by the world, what you stand for and against, what you believe and what is unique about you. It is the part of someone's mind that you own, or the part that makes you the go-to person or company in your industry, both in terms of your message and the mechanisms and media that deliver that message.

The 4th C, Communication, is delivered through:
- *Legacy*
- *Purpose*
- *Brand (YOU)*
- *Marketing*
- *Sales*
- *Public speaking*
- *Reputation*
- *Referrals*

Legacy

Here's a reminder of legacy from chapter 1:

Legacy answers the question *'Did you matter?'*

Legacy is the memory of you. It is what's left of you after you are gone. It is the difference you made while you were here and how you helped develop mankind. It is your dent in the universe. Without legacy you were nothing but worm food. Without legacy you have no purpose to fulfil and you have no direction in life. You float down someone else's stream blown by someone else's wind. Legacy is your epitaph. The torch carried by others from your funeral and how long it lasts afterwards.

Purpose

Here's a reminder of purpose from chapter 1:

Your purpose is how you deliver and fulfil your legacy.

For most my life I have struggled with:

"Why am I here?"

"What am I supposed to do?"

I did many courses on having direction in life, discovering meaning and purpose and finding my true calling. The reality is that most of what I finally found out I already knew (and all of it I already was but was afraid to express). I was looking for some kind of permission from someone else. In the end you know when you know! Just make sure you find the time to work on this, so you don't wait your whole life. Don't wait for the event, make the event.

Having purpose for a human being comes primarily from being productive and needed in some way. The real enemy is boredom. Having purpose is living your legacy in the now, doing what you are meant to do, being in flow and allowing yourself to grow through the process while contributing in a positive way to your environment.

What I find fascinating is that once some people have become wealthy, they feel compelled to give back and help others. It's part of who we are as human beings; it's in our collective Wealth DNA. And it gives purpose and meaning to the giver. A life alone with no giving or assisting fellow man has no purpose. To be really fulfilling, the purpose has to be bigger than you.

Brand (YOU)

Brand (YOU) is you becoming known for your legacy living through purpose. It isn't just your brand, it is how you are known, remembered and then shared by everyone. It is how fast the message of YOU spreads. It is what you are known for personally and in business. It is your legacy manifesting into the minds of your friends, network and customers. It is your values being lived and inspiring others to be those values. It is what you stand for and what you stand against. It is what is human and accessible and real and honest and authentic about you as seen by others. It is your tagline or foundational phrase. It's that little bit of space for the thing that you do that you own in the minds of others.

Brand YOU is part of your intangible collateral that creates loyalty to you. It is what/who falls in love with you and gets people promoting you without asking for commissions. It is what you have in common with your audience or network, it is what makes them relate to you or want to be more like you. Affinity with Brand YOU comes from common history, common values and common goals and vision. Only if you communicate them clearly can you do justice to your purpose.

Marketing

Marketing is the message and the channels and different media for that message in which you spread your purpose and brand. If your legacy is a chain of shops and your (personal, current) purpose is to serve the customer in the shop, then marketing is getting people in the shop in the first place.

Marketing is both the content and the context of your message. Marketing is understanding your ideal customers wants, needs, pains, fears and desires, and sharing a message in a way they relate to that inspires them to act or change. It is every word written and visual language on your website or brochure and the delivery of your values through these vehicles. It is your strapline and promise, your mission statement and your "About Me" page. It is the contents of your Facebook and Twitter profiles, the connections on your LinkedIn profile and the photo history of Instagram. It is the wording and imagery of your adverts, editorials, business cards and flyers.

The delivery mechanisms for your marketing are now so global and inter-connected, setting up and growing your business and brand is easier than ever. You can join Facebook, LinkedIn, Twitter, Skype, Instagram and YouTube for free, as well as many other social media and marketing platforms. You can virtually and instantly connect with anyone across the globe through voice, text, photo and video. You can join communities as fast as you can search for them. You can access tens of thousands of like-minded people and customers at the click of a "Like" or an "Add." You can upload your messages to the world as quick as your Internet connection. And you can do all of this from anywhere in the world, day and night, night and day.

You could be the best guitarist in the world, but if no one sees you play, you don't exist. Susan Boyle got seen by hundreds of millions thanks to YouTube. The Arctic Monkeys built their fan base almost fully online before they became mainstream. Once out of a record contract, Radiohead sold their next album without a record label and allowed you to choose what to pay, on a simple web page anyone could set up.

A quirky video could get your website 1 million or more hits. One Twitter share from a celebrity wearing your products could launch your business into the big time. You can offer amazing instant customer service through Facebook private messages or online virtual meetings. You can set up an online shop on EBay or Amazon or your own website and drive huge amounts of traffic to it using online marketing media, most of it free. Or you can advertise by paying per click on Google, Amazon, Facebook and Twitter paid advertising platforms and target hordes of hungry buyers. You can self-publish your book and launch it across social and business platforms and become a best seller in a day.

And on top of all that magic you can outsource nearly all of it to someone sitting on their computer in another country who you pay by the hour or by the job to do it all for you. So even if you don't know how, you can still achieve the results using leverage and outsourcing.

Sales

If your legacy is a chain of shops and your (personal, current) purpose is to serve the customer in the shop, and marketing is getting people in the shop in the first place, then selling is not letting them leave without spending some (or all) of their money.

Sales is the manifestation of legacy living through purpose, brand and marketing into money in the bank. Sales is getting the customer or JV partner or investor to say yes and wire the money to you or your solicitor. Sales is the persuasion part of the process, influencing someone to do what you want them to do, having them believe it was their decision and thanking you for it.

Sales is transferring your passion, enthusiasm and energy to the other person in a way that inspires them to buy. Sales is reducing their risk, giving someone certainty of a result or outcome, consistent with the brand and marketing promise, and making it easy for them to spend their money with you or make the buying decision.

Sales is highlighting a problem or need and giving the cure or solution, overcoming the fears or objections along the way in a comfortable environment. Sales is being a leader showing others what they need and caring for them along the journey of discovery. Successful sales is giving someone certainty that the decision they are about to make is the right one for them and letting results be the proof.

Whoever believes the most in sale, wins. If someone choses not to buy from you, they sold you better on why they shouldn't have your product, service or idea. They convinced you, and you agreed. So it's sell or be sold to, all day, every day: ideas, beliefs, life plans, goods and services.

Sales is congruent when it comes from legacy and purpose. No one feels right about selling something they don't believe in or that they think the customer or recipient doesn't want or need. But when sales comes from legacy and purpose, you know the only right thing for them is to do it, because you believe in it so much because it is an extension of who you are and what legacy you are here to live out. That's why you should learn sales and influence skills, because if you believe your product or service truly changes lives, you should do whatever you can to sell it.

Public Speaking

Your public speaking ability is how you inspire your legacy and purpose in others.

In fact, many of the most famous leaders of the world were/are also the greatest orators. And it's not just great leverage to be able to speak to hundreds or thousands of people at the same time, it's also a very highly paid skill (and therefor worth studying and learning). Many politicians or celebrities get paid £50,000 to £350,000 for a public speech. I spoke alongside Lord Sugar at the 2011 Property Superconference in London, and his fees were in that range for less than an hour's Q&A. He didn't even have a PowerPoint presentation!

You might never had a desire to be on stage and become a public speaker or you might have secretly wanted to be one. Whatever the case may be, you have to try it. I teach public speaking, and there are so many cases of reluctant students who end up loving it and having deep transformational experiences. And in my case it's one of the things I really treasure and enjoy in my life.

One of the most effective and powerful ways to share your message is as a professional public speaker. Anyone can speak in public, but most don't realise how much they are damaging their brand by doing so poorly.

Your ability to speak in public and inspire your purpose in others transcends all media. You could be on a stage at Wealth Breakthrough Live (we are looking for trainers to help us live our purpose, so if you would love to be a speaker/trainer please get in touch on the Wealth DNA Facebook group), you could be recording a video for the homepage of your website or YouTube, you could be pitching to a JV partner or investor for funds for your business or property, you could be selling one to one or one to many, you could be networking, or you could be creating a compelling case for someone to go on a date with you. All of these are in essence aspects of public speaking – the conscious craft of using words and body language to influence one to many.

I never knew I would become a professional public speaker. In fact I wasn't very good at it and totally scared of it. I was not confident in most areas of my life, so the last thing I wanted to do was to get on a stage and embarrass myself in front of hundreds of people. No thank you, sir. But I soon realised that the people making all the money in my initial niche of Internet marketing were all great speakers getting all the big stages and leveraging their time selling one to many –

sometimes thousands and making tens of thousands of pounds in just an hour! Some of them didn't necessarily know more than I did on internet marketing, they just knew how to present their message more effectively to more customers in less time.

Summary

The fourth C, communication, is the vehicle and outlet for the other three Cs: cashflow, collateral and character. It is the way you live your legacy through purpose in relation to the rest of the planet, the advertising of you to receive all the gifts the world has to offer. But you have to be visible. If the world doesn't know you exist and what your gift and your message is, people can't follow you and people can't buy from you. And the more people you can effortlessly reach (the size of your audience) the more money you can effortlessly make.

Communication instructs the world what you want to manifest and is the portal between thoughts and feelings and the results you receive from them. Master communicators rule and lead the world, because they can translate their legacy in a compelling way for others to see vision through it and become part of it.

So communication is about just two things. Know exactly what you want to say. Learn how to say it well!

Summary Of The 4 Cs

So there we have it, the four Cs of the Wealth Diamond and the secret for changing your Wealth DNA and the proven principles of lasting wealth. Here's the Wealth Diamond once again:

The 4 Cs are four parts of a whole. The diamond has its perfect shape, and all four areas need to be fully developed for the diamond to have its highest value. We mentioned a few times that a diamond is nothing more than a piece of charcoal that in the right environment handled pressure extremely well. Choose that right environment and learn how to handle pressure from an empowering and supportive peer group and mentors who have what you want to have, do what you want to do and be who you want to be.

Wealth DNA proposes that anyone, and that includes you, can change the 4 Cs that make up your value in the free market economy. As wealth is what we all desire, the 4 Cs will deliver it into your life – guaranteed. Dig deep to find what stirs you and what holds you back and then allow the laws of the universe to do their bit. Mainly being damn slow at manifesting what you want! (Just joking – I'm not complaining!)

If you got this far in the book, then I want to personally thank you for having spent time with me. I really do hope that you found the discourse useful and instructive. That you will take things from the book that will change how you think or how you act in the world and that the notion of Wealth DNA and the Wealth Diamond are now models you use as references to navigate through life on your way to personal fulfilment and financial freedom.

Wealth DNA

212

Conclusion

So now it's time to act. Get on the journey. Make some changes. Change your Wealth DNA. Once you get started and see the first results, you won't want to stop. It's your individual journey to freedom, and not just financial freedom. As I'm writing these lines in the mall of the emirates in Dubai, having spent the last week in a five-star resort sharing with you what changed my life from delivering pizzas in Slough to living the dream, I feel humbled. Humbled to get the opportunity to share this important knowledge with you, this information, which for some strange reason is obscured and not as easily accessible as it should be in the world. I feel humbled by the fact that you have entrusted me with accepting my experience and my insights as signposts to your own journey to fulfillment.

Whatever it is you want to achieve, you're not alone. We are out there. Unreasonable people who want it all: wealth and happiness. Love and money. And we help each other. We have created communities and classes, workshops and workouts, strategies and support systems. Join us. It'll be epic.

It's important you start the journey. Time is short. No matter how much you'll leverage, in the end we all run out of time. And it doesn't matter what you believe will happen after your time on this planet - your time on this planet is limited. So use it. Do something you're proud of. Don't settle for mediocrity. You don't have to.

Start small and dream big. Let the miracle of compounding and the laws of momentum work for you. There's more than enough money in the world for us all to be multi-millionaires, so someone's got your money! Go and give, create, share and love and you will manifest all the wealth you desire.

So Here Is What I Want You To Do Next...

Make a commitment to yourself and then let the world know that you are on the journey to change your Wealth DNA - to move yourself from the dependence of earned income to the freedom of

streams and streams of leveraged passive recurring income.

Currently you might get 90 or 100 per cent of your income from your time and efforts; start to reduce the dependency. Build vehicles of wealth. Buy assets and invest in yourself. Do whatever it takes but start the journey. Now.

How do you know you're on the right track? When your percentage of earned income decreases, you know you're winning. Every step is progress. Every per cent counts.

So make a public pledge on our Facebook page and join the hundreds of people from around the world who have decided to change their Wealth DNA. It's easy and it's powerful. A public commitment to let the world know you made a decision. Search Wealth DNA now and make a public commitment; we are there to help you every step of the way.

I feel I'm on a mission. And that feeling gives me legacy and purpose. May you find yours. I hope our paths will cross one day.